THE
SCARLET
SHAMROCK

JOHN MURPHY

ISBN: 1489598863
ISBN-13: 9781489598868

Library of Congress Control Number: 2013910242
CreateSpace Independent Publishing Platform
North Charleston, South Carolina

Stranger, if you travel into the land of the Spartans,
tell them we lie here obedient to their laws.

– Epitaph left at Thermopylae in
480 B.C. by Spartan warriors.

PREFACE

The 20th Century gave rise to some of the most hideous confrontations known to man. The destruction and loss of lives brought on by two world wars stagger the imagination. Yet sandwiched within this time period, arose on a lesser scale, two equally vicious and lengthy conflicts. They were the Irish "Troubles" and the Vietnam War.

Ireland and Vietnam shared a common quest for independence. Because invaders had ignited their hatred, their causes made for two of the more complex and extended confrontations of the last century.

"The Troubles" in Ireland emanated from the Plantation Era in 1603. Irish chieftains, exiled from the northern Rathmullen area, made way for settlers from England who took their lands.

England, shortly thereafter, established the Irish Society, akin to the Virginia Society in the New World. Both represented wealthy London companies which had a charter to colonize and civilize both Ireland and America. Both began by dividing the lands among them.

But the problem wasn't just the London companies. Scots sailed across the North Channel and seized the lands on the Ards Peninsula on the northeast coast of Ulster. These settlers were Presbyterians, not the Anglicans associated with the Plantation Era. And they showed a greater sense of independence than the English.

The Scots had more success than the Irish Society. They gained footholds all across Ulster. In 1641, the Gaelic Irish and the Catholic regions of Ireland rebelled. They protested the confiscation of their lands and the advent of a different people, religion, commerce and government. Trinity University in Dublin houses 32 volumes which record the slaughter and deprivation brought on by the rebellion.

Eight years later, Oliver Cromwell, Lord Protector of England, invaded Ireland and pillaged the country. He attacked both English Catholic Royalists and Irish rebels, and he ruthlessly put down their rebellion.

Cromwell sowed the seeds of rage which have lasted for over 300 years.

Similarly, half-way around the world, the French in 1787 began to make inroads into what was to become French Indochina.

The Japanese conquered the region in World War II only to have it revert to French control after the war. But warfare continued. Vietnamese nationalists sought to unify the country, and they battled the French, then the Americans, and finally, when the Americans went home, they overwhelmed the abandoned South Vietnamese to achieve it.

This story takes place within the cauldron of these two diverse encounters.

ACKNOWLEDGMENTS

I want to thank several persons for their assistance in this book. First and foremost is Colonel Billy Spangler, US Army (Ret). A gifted writer and teacher, he provided the critical guidance and encouragement needed to bring this novel to fruition. Additionally, two of my ever-constant sons, Kevin, a busy Washington, D.C. attorney, and Michael, a retired Army Lieutenant Colonel, took time to artfully edit their father's work. And their pithy comments gave it clarity.

Next are Dr. Bernadette McNulty, a superior educator and editor who finely tuned the book, and Major General Ted Hopgood USMC (Ret) my former battalion executive officer and trusted friend, who supplied me with pragmatic and professional insights.

Finally, I want to thank my other two very accomplished children, daughter Maureen and son Mark for their support, and my wife Joan, whose patience with and understanding of a writer's need for isolation allowed for me to complete the work.

CHAPTER 1

Major Spencer Cattley liked his work. As a finance officer, he epitomized his calling—precise, accurate and dedicated. He fit British army historian John Keegan's description of the warrior: "Some men can be nothing but soldiers." And Spencer knew this. So content was he in his profession that he never thought of life outside the army.

But despite his obvious military fit, there was something wrong.

Cattley had no friends—only acquaintances. He was a loner. No one really knew much about him.

The 33 year old major had graduated from the Royal Military Academy at Sandhurst in 1953. The Korean War was winding down, but he didn't serve there. Instead, he went straight into the finance field and stayed in England throughout his career.

He studied accounting before entering the army and had a command of both numbers and details. These qualities served him well at Sandhurst and later in his various army assignments. Fortunately, they stood out and overshadowed his lackluster abilities in marksmanship, physical training, and close order drill.

Cattley looked good in uniform. His wooden presence, accentuated by a six-foot, 175 pound frame and classic features, was capped by a full head of sandy colored hair and hazel eyes.

He might have appropriately graced a recruiting poster, but his long, slender hands seemed out of place. They were not those of a soldier but rather the hands of an artisan or musician—more comfortable with a palette than a pistol. In a way, they complimented his tenor voice.

All this aside, the army had provided him structure and exactness. He needed both because without them he became unduly anxious and agitated.

Spencer's early life probably contributed to this personality trait because he didn't grow up in an ordinary family. He was a lonely child. He had no siblings, and his impressionable years were shaped by the odd relationship his parents endured. They were detached. Although they went through the motions of being married, they shared no intimacy. They had drifted apart and resembled two boarders under the same roof.

His mother was a strikingly beautiful brunette with almond-shaped blue eyes. Her chiseled features resembled a delicately carved Greek sculpture. She knew how to keep herself radiant and always looked as if she had stepped from a fashion magazine. Women watched her with envy, and men simply gaped at her.

Despite her physical beauty, she was a dour person. She showed little warmth and affection to anyone. Instead, she went about her daily routine, oblivious to her only child and her obnoxious husband. She would clean incessantly and would repeatedly check things she'd already done. Driven by some silent demon, she washed her hands multiple times each day and kept them raw and inflamed.

Her smile was mechanical and unnerving. It gave one the impression that somehow her physical and inner being were unconnected.

When the family dined, she would pick at her food and seldom spoke.

Conversely, Cattley's highly analytical and obese father dominated any conversation, and that usually centered on his bank job. Neither his wife nor his son showed any interest in his babblings and spent their meals in silence.

The elder Cattley was as ugly as his wife was beautiful. He had an odd shaped head on which nothing seemed to fit. The eyes were set too close, his ears too big, his nose too long and hooked, and his stubby teeth were lost behind a large, puffy mouth that held a fixed grin.

Despite his physical and social drawbacks, Cattley's father knew how to make money, and he provided his wife and son a comfortable life.

Spencer Cattley often had flashbacks about his unhappy childhood and an emotional event that left him shaken.

First, his father, the ever efficient know-it-all banker, committed suicide. It appears bank regulators found a number of improprieties in his financial transactions and were about to bring charges against him. Bank officials had put him on administrative leave until they could resolve the gambling and theft allegations that surrounded him.

The strain became too great, and the man stuck a shotgun in his mouth and pulled the trigger.

Spencer found his father when he returned from classes that day. His mother was home too; however, her indifference to her husband's death shocked the young man as much as the tragedy itself. That's because she was more intent on cleaning up the mess than expressing any horror or sorrow over the incident.

The next day, she entered a mental institution, and Spencer Cattley never saw her again—by design.

Like all men, Cattley had his own flaws. His exactness bordered on the obsessive, and he constantly guarded against anyone taking him for some Little Lord Fauntleroy. But still his interest heightened in his Worthy Down office in Winchester, south of London when he received the stranger's call. The stranger said he needed to meet with him on a matter of utmost importance to the major's future. Cattley felt intimidated by the caller's voice. It was deep, assertive and menacing. It sounded Celtic, maybe Welsh or Scottish, but he wasn't sure because the gravelly texture masked its origin.

Regardless, the party came across authoritatively in contrast to the major's fastidious manner.

Spencer's first reaction was to dismiss the caller and tell him that he didn't have time for games and wasn't interested in pranks or threatening calls...and that he could officially correspond with him through regular channels.

"This is no prank," the stranger went on, "It's about Barcelona."

Cattley froze. The stranger's words petrified him as old memories and fears became almost real again. Like an emotional tsunami, an ominous sense swept over him as he reluctantly agreed to a luncheon meeting.

Preoccupied throughout his morning duties, Spencer wanted the encounter over. True, his established competency and professionalism had allowed him to deal in very sensitive fiscal matters surrounding covert operations, but such were always within the army structure. Now it was Barcelona. What did the stranger know, and why had he singled him out?

"I might be a bit late this afternoon," he told his secretary when he left his office at 11:30 A.M. that fateful March day in 1967.

Outside, he turned left into a typical cold spring mist and briskly walked two blocks and turned north for another four blocks to the Fremantle Inn where the stranger had said he'd meet him. Descending to its adjoining lower level pub, he immediately went to the bar and ordered whiskey.

As he stood waiting for his appointment, with the whiskey warming his guts, the major reflected on his army career of 14 years and how quickly it had passed. He sometimes compared himself to a monk—selfless and dedicated to his calling. He'd never married...gave his all to queen and country.

Though deep in thought, he came to attention as a low, rasping voice uttered, "Major Cattley?" Spencer turned slowly and came face to face with a large well-groomed, yet rough-looking man. His beard was salt and pepper and although neatly trimmed, seemed so thick that it overpowered his face...but it was the eyes of the stranger that held him. A piercing light blue, like marble, and without warmth, they emitted an underlying fierceness.

Spencer overcame his initial paralyzing silence and stiffly responded, "Yes, I am Major Cattley."

"Shall we move to the corner booth?" the bearded stranger asked. Walking machinelike to the empty booth, the major followed. He wondered why he was even there.

Cattley decided to go on the offensive. He politely but firmly suggested his time was limited and hoped the business wouldn't take long. Just as well let the stranger know who was calling the shots. Spencer thought, I'll give him some rope before I shut him off. No harm in listening, though. He sat down facing the stranger.

"What'll you chaps have?" a portly waitress asked. Cattley ordered a pint and a bowl of fish chowder.

The stranger, almost inaudibly, said he wanted the same. The waitress left.

Feeling like he'd sort of taken charge, Cattley again pushed ahead. "I'd like to know who you are, sir. You don't sound like a Londoner. Are you making a long stay?"

The man paused for a lengthy period and without any sign of emotion simply said, "My name is irrelevant. What matters is that I'm an intermediary for the Irish Republican Army."

"You're what?

"I have no time for this rubbish; I'm—"

"Before you go tripping off major, I'd suggest you pay close attention to what I have to say about you and what the IRA needs from you. Should you not listen, I can promise that you'll be finished in your bloody army."

"You have a different accent; I don't understand your IRA association," Major Cattley said, puzzled. "And how do I fit into the equation?"

"First, major, many Anglo-Irish, whether Catholic or Protestant, support both the unification of Ireland and the independence of Scotland. Secondly, the IRA needs information which only you can provide. And you will provide it."

The stranger's subdued and deliberate delivery continued to unnerve the flustered officer.

Spencer tried again to regain control. "I say, you seem rather sure of yourself. What makes you so confident I have what you need or that I would give it to you? If it's money you want, my good fellow, forget it. Go rob a bank!"

Unperturbed by the major's insult, the stranger coldly focused on his mission. "The IRA has suffered since the failed 1956 Troubles. Its ranks have thinned out. Despite the scarcity of active members, those who remain are more dedicated and determined than ever to make all of Ireland one nation.

"But a problem stands in the IRA's way; it needs a capable informant. The army has attempted several small forays since 1956, and each time one of its boys ends up a corpse or a British ambush blows the whole operation. If there is a mole, and we strongly suspect there is, then he is on the take and you're secretly paying him. The IRA knows the British Army engages in such activities around the world and that operatives receive payment from your office.

"Bluntly, Major Cattley, we want you to provide this mole's name—nothing more."

The chunky waitress, bulging from her undersized uniform, shuffled to the booth and served the ale and fish chowder the men had ordered.

Placing a napkin in his lap and blowing on a spoonful of steaming chowder, Cattley, in an almost unconcerned tone and not looking at the stranger, said, "And what if I don't give you a name?"

"Then the British Army will discharge you, major. They will do it because you are a closet homosexual, and you know as well as I do that homosexuals cannot serve in the British forces. You either cooperate with the IRA or it will expose you...no pun intended," he smiled.

Cattley could feel the color draining from his face. He was visibly shaken. Trying to gain his composure, his tightened throat managed a high-pitched "You can never prove such an accusation!"

"Yes we can, major," the stranger said confidently. "We too have operatives, and one told us he thought you might be gay. We've watched you for almost two years now. We know you take holiday alone on the continent. You lose yourself in large cities and carefully surface in closely guarded homosexual establishments.

"Our operatives finally lucked out in Barcelona. Through their contacts in the gay community, they paid for compromising photographs of you, major. You see, many people will scrap their principles: IRA moles recruited by your army, many homosexual club owners, and yes, even you, major."

At that point, the stranger took a very clear black and white photograph from an envelope and showed it to Cattley.

Embarrassed, shaken and without defense, Cattley's head fell backwards and he drew labored breaths and expelled them through puckered lips.

"Will you work with us, major?" the stranger asked, as a slight smile crossed his lips.

Cattley could not believe what was happening. He'd been so careful in the few indiscretions he'd allowed himself in the gratification of his weakness. To realize he'd been tracked, spied upon and caught violating the crown's special trust devastated him. At that moment he saw himself for what he really was—a fraud. He'd always felt inferior to his fellow officers but compensated for it by parading as a fiscal authority.

The conversation ended as quickly as it started. Cattley sat mesmerized and dumbfounded.

"Give it some thought, major," the bearded man said. "I'll contact you Monday next. At that time we can finalize arrangements for the name I want. If not, the IRA will forward to your superiors a definitive package of your unauthorized conduct. I advise you that the picture I showed you is just the tip of the iceberg. We have multiple photos and depositions from the parties involved. It's overwhelming evidence, major; there isn't any way you can beat it. I'll take care of the bill on my way out." The stranger rose and left.

"You all right, soldier?" the waitress asked, displaying a frozen grin on big, loose lips.

Startled, Spencer looked up at the fat woman and then around the empty pub. Obviously, she wanted to finish cleaning and leave. The ship's clock behind the bar chimed three bells (1:30 P.M.) as Spencer slid from the booth and left the pub.

It had turned colder. An icy wind bit into his face as he walked back to his office, still dazed. His self-confidence was gone. He nearly hated himself.

Dorothy Pound, his somewhat coy secretary, inquired about his ashen appearance and the meeting. He shrugged her off, went into his office and closed the door.

It was Friday. Spencer had an invitation to an Indian Embassy party in London that evening. Each year a select number of British officers from the respective services received invitations to such parties, and Spencer's superiors suggested he attend.

He called his immediate superior, Colonel Drumford, and advised him he was ill and had to cancel. He knew his excuse was lame and that the colonel really didn't believe him.

Miss Pound left precisely at 5:00 P.M. She bade her sullen boss a pleasant weekend and exited the building. Spencer sat with the same empty stare fixed upon the blank wall he faced.

He left his office at 6:00 P.M. and walked one mile south to his orderly apartment located on the top floor of a six-story building.

Primarily well-to-do middle-aged couples occupied the one and two bedroom apartments. Little noise resonated in the clean hallways and most of the occupants kept to themselves. Cattley had lived there 10 years, and it fit his lifestyle perfectly.

Spencer's closets contained few clothes, mostly military uniforms. His Spartan furnishings lent no warmth to the rooms.

He had two bedrooms, one of which he made into an office. He spent many evenings and weekends there, where he studied army fiscal regulations and figured new approaches to military-related pay matters.

His efforts paid off. His superiors repeatedly praised his plans and implemented many of them, all the while ignoring his nit-picking manner.

The living room had a sofa, leather reclining chair and a small television. Bookshelves lined one wall.

The kitchen too was small, but there was room for a table and four chairs. Cattley ate most of his meals at it.

A lone picture hung in the living room—that of Queen Elizabeth. No remembrances of his parents, home, school or acquaintances turned up in the other rooms.

Cattley's apartment resembled an operating room—neat and sterile.

Immediately after he came into the entryway, he hung up his coat and went into the bedroom where he changed into his robe. He then went directly to the kitchen and reached into the upper cabinet over the sink to take down bottles of Scotch whiskey, sweet vermouth, bitters and Maraschino cherries. They composed the ingredients of his favorite mixed drink—a Rob Roy.

He measured two shots of whiskey, half a shot of vermouth, and a dash of bitters into a beaker. He then swirled two cherries around in the container along with some crushed ice. He poured the contents into a cocktail glass and retired to his easy chair.

Cattley had a selective taste in Scotch whiskies. He despised the blended brands shipped throughout the world and considered them nothing more than bilge water.

True Scotch drinkers, in his mind, drank only single malt whiskies, not blends. His favorite was 16 year old Dalwhinnie. It came from the Highlands and had a smooth, smoky malt flavor.

Exact in his routine, Cattley allowed himself no more than two drinks a day, but today would be an exception.

He sat in his easy chair. The subdued light coming into his apartment windows outlined his rigid posture as Spencer mechanically lifted the Waterford crystal to his lips. The expensive Scotch whiskey, with a touch of sweet vermouth, brought him the only pleasure he'd experienced this Friday.

He savored each sip of the Rob Roy as he mentally reviewed the happenings of the day. He questioned how he would deal with his latest adversary. The bearded stranger had changed his whole life. No longer could he live in the stable and controlled environment of his military lifestyle. Gone was the security he enjoyed and had so badly needed.

On his way to finishing a third drink, the telephone rang. "Major Cattley, Colonel Drumford here. I say old chap, feeling any better?" Spencer's already flushed face reddened even more. Angered by the obvious check on his integrity, he advised his colonel he was coping. He wanted to tell him to mind his own business, but he could only think such thoughts. He felt his curt answer betrayed a slight hint of intoxication.

Cattley didn't want to create more trouble than he'd already had this day, so he thanked the colonel for his concern and immediately hung up.

The hours drifted by as the disturbed officer continued to drink. He'd switched from Rob Roys to straight shots. He poured them into a Riedel designed single malt Scotch glass made of Austrian Tyrol lead crystal. His thoughts, blurred and convoluted now, gave him no solace as he passed into unconsciousness.

Saturday seemed little different from Friday night. When awake, Cattley kept drinking but ate little food. By that night, he'd just about convinced himself that suicide would provide the solution to his new troubles.

Maybe it ran in the family. His father faced a similar crisis and ended his life. And his mother had lost her way too. Could their combination of feral genes doom him also? Would anybody really care? He had no relatives or friends who'd experience shock or sorrow by his deed. He concluded that his life meant nothing to anyone except himself.

Would he use a pistol, sleeping pills, or maybe even his beloved Rob Roys? Falling in front of a speeding tram would be a more secretive demise than a bullet or drink.

Spencer would choose neither because he was a coward. He knew he could not muster the courage to kill himself. He never considered the propriety of the deed because he lacked any moral fiber.

Instead, he rationalized his conflict by comparing himself to two of England's famous military poets in the First World War: Wilfred Owen and Siegfried Sassoon. Both won the Military Cross for bravery and both allegedly dallied in homosexual relationships. Owens didn't survive the war; Sassoon did.

Time, being a great healer, provided Spencer a solution by Sunday afternoon. He'd decided he would cooperate with the IRA. Because obvious risks came with such a decision, he would likewise put demands on the IRA just as they had placed on him. He actually saw in this ugly confrontation a chance to make money. "Yes, I will oblige them, and I will win the day," he whispered over the mouth of his cocktail glass.

Relieved and confident in his decision, Spencer went to work Monday as if nothing unusual had happened. Colonel Drumford made no follow-up query about Spencer's illness, nor did Spencer mention the subject.

Precise as usual, but preoccupied, Cattley waded through his morning ritual of tabulating pay accounts and auditing army unit records. At 10:00 A.M. Miss Pound advised him that a man identified only as an acquaintance wished to speak with him.

There was no mistaking the stranger's voice. "We'll meet this evening at the Paupers' Pub. Make it 7:00 P.M." Without another word, the phone went silent.

Strangely, Spencer felt no fear as he put the phone down. He even looked forward to the meeting. It offered a challenge—the most exciting he'd ever known.

He would soon be living on the sharp edge of financial success or professional ruination. It would be nothing new for Spencer to take on another facade; he'd deceived the army for years with his covert homosexual activities. He felt confident he could continue deceiving it by secretly working with the IRA. He knew the intermediary would not jeopardize a critical intelligence source by unmasking him. And besides, what they did to the unfortunate bloke who was ratting on IRA operations didn't concern him in the least. Only money and the preservation of his military status mattered at this point.

The officer left work on time and went directly home where he changed into a green tweed sport coat, white turtleneck sweater and tan corduroy slacks. He then walked the three miles to the Paupers' Pub. He needed the fresh air and exercise to ease the remnants of the weekend hangover.

The Paupers' Pub resembled its name only in its rustic appearance. Darkly stained hardwood floors with wide, slightly undulating boards gave an unsure footing to the first time visitor. Half a dozen tables dotted the interior. Opposite the entrance, a massive bar with numerous stools stretched fifteen feet along the far wall. Indirect lighting added to the somber appearance and reinforced the savage appearance of the big game heads mounted in the room.

When Cattley entered the pub a few minutes before the hour, he hesitated momentarily. He looked about and focused on a hunched figure. Spencer didn't see the stranger any place else in the pub, and figured it must be he.

He walked over to the table and asked the man if he could join him. The burly figure turned; he was the stranger. Without fanfare, he motioned for Cattley to sit.

The two men momentarily looked at each other and then Spencer spoke. "I'm ready to deal," he said in an upbeat tone. The stranger smiled faintly and waited. Taking it as a cue to continue, Spencer assertively and carefully spoke his mind. "I say, the IRA asks a great deal of me. I'm well aware that I'm negotiating from a weak power base, but still I believe I'm due some consideration and all that. I have information critical to your needs. Without it, the IRA cannot operate with certainty. Should I refuse to cooperate and am forced to leave the army, someone, who will not cooperate with you, will take my job...and you lose. Thus, I'm your only hope. You need me, and I need you."

The stranger looked at him with a puzzled expression. "How do you need the IRA, other than to not disclose your tendencies?"

Cattley looked confidently into the stranger's eyes and said, "I need monetary compensation. This information is very valuable, and I think you should give a good account of yourself and reward my cooperation."

The faint smile left the stranger's bearded face. He squinted in a perplexed fashion and stoically asked, "How much compensation did you have in mind, major?"

He shot back, "Ten-thousand pounds," giving the obvious impression that he had calculated the worth of his information.

The stranger looked at him with a blank expression. Spencer didn't know if he'd caught him off guard or angered him.,

The IRA operative took a long drink from the pint in front of him, set it down and said, "I will give you five-thousand pounds right now for the name. Take it or leave it. Future names will warrant double that." The IRA had rightly deduced that Cattley would want money.

Spencer took an envelope from his coat pocket and removed a photocopy of a pay voucher. It was marked TOP SECRET and was made out for five-thousand pounds to a Sean McGinty; he handed it to the stranger.

The bearded man's mouth fell open as he looked at the document. He knew the informant and his facial contortions gave away the shock and disappointment he felt. He rolled his eyes back and slowly shook his head.

"Are you all right, my good man?" Spencer asked.

"Aye...I am," the stranger replied.

As he recovered his composure, he too reached into his coat and removed an envelope. He handed it to the major. "All the money is there. I expect that if other names surface, you will advise me of them when I periodically contact you. Thank you for your cooperation. I'm glad that we can work together."

Hatred, nationalism and greed formed the only bonds these men had. Neither made the move to shake hands as they rose and departed the pub.

Before they went their different ways, Spencer raised a caveat. "I ask that the document I gave you be held in the strictest confidence. Should it or knowledge of it reach British authorities, I'm finished as your informant."

The stranger removed the photocopy from his coat and gave it back to Cattley. "This should allow you to rest easily.

I needed only the name. The voucher convinced me of its validity. We'll protect you, major, be assured--just don't cross us."

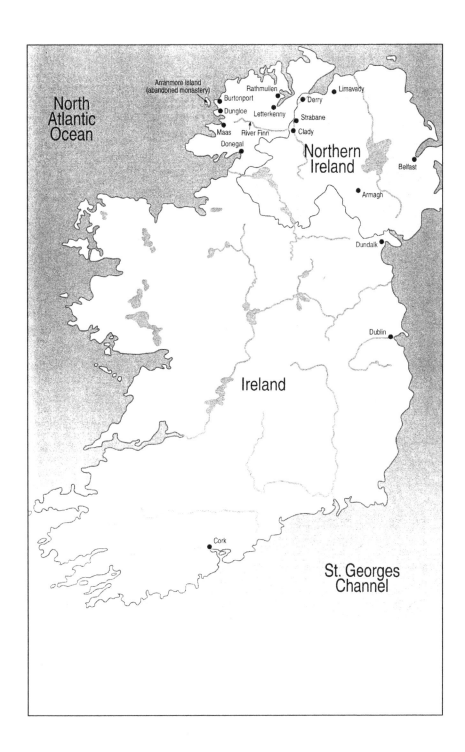

North
Atlantic
Ocean

Arranmore Island
(abandoned monastery)
Burtonport
Dungloe
Rathmullen
Letterkenny
Derry
Limavady
Strabane
Maas
River Finn
Clady
Donegal

Northern
Ireland

Belfast

Armagh

Dundalk

Dublin

Ireland

Cork

St. Georges
Channel

CHAPTER 2

Clady, Northern Ireland.

As Major Spencer Cattley and the stranger lunched for the first time on Friday afternoon, another meeting was about to take place. It also pitted two adversaries of similar persuasion.

Clady lies 380 miles northwest across the Irish Sea from the Fremantle Inn.

Population 860.

A handful of single and two-story white and gray stone buildings line the poorly paved road that winds down to the River Finn. There it crosses on a single lane, stone bridge, consisting of six Romanesque arches, into County Donegal in the Irish Republic.

The sound of a hammer striking metal on an anvil rings like an off-key church bell. The laughter of children floats across the meadows like the white bed sheets swaying gently from a line behind the third house on the right. Beyond it, a few head of Hereford cattle loll on the grassy hillsides.

The people here live simple lives. Their living comes from the land, a land handed down from one generation to another. So too is their Irish language continued. They speak its melodious tones in soft rhythms, especially when they gather at Moran's Pub on Saturday evenings.

Clady's men folk spin yarns of crops and animals, children and grandchildren. Sometimes yarns of youth and manhood remembered. And, as their evening lengthens, of how their town fought for the Republicans in the Irish Civil War. A few speak in hushed tones of their participation in the 1956 Troubles—the term used to describe the recurrent violence between Catholics and Protestants over discrimination and the manipulation of voting districts. Still younger men roll their sleeves to show with pride more recent scars.

Their women sit at a corner table. They talk of babies and women's things. Their high-pitched laughter causes the men to turn and look, then shake their heads, before returning to their interrupted conversation. That conversation leads to the bridge. The men's recollections are punctuated with laughter as they relive the memory of British frustration at the IRA "Flying Columns" that slashed across the border in hit-and-run raids on key British installations. Unable to find and apprehend the guilty, the British army retaliated. They demolished the Clady Bridge three times since 1922.

Its people promptly rebuilt it.

On the surface, Clady looked like so many Irish villages — serene and tranquil. Nothing more than another picture postcard in a tourist office display.

But looks are often deceiving.

Clady was a hotbed for IRA activities.

The British Army periodically ventured back to Clady with B-Special patrols, but did little more than make their presence known. The IRA would periodically snipe at them and the local populace would passively show their resentment.

Morale among the British fell because they saw no hope of winning. They felt constrained because they could only fight a reactionary war.

Their more erudite commanders recognized an emerging analogy between the Americans in Vietnam and the French before them.

However, this particular Friday seemed different. British authorities had dispatched several Special Air Service (SAS) combat target reconnaissance teams (CRTs) to the Clady region. An intelligence source had purported that IRA operatives were active in the area. This raised concerns that the enemy was establishing weapons caches for future raids on Strabane and Londonderry further to the north.

The SAS had a fearsome reputation, which included taking no prisoners. When things became dicey and the IRA over confident, the SAS would appear. Often the results were gruesome, both for the IRA and the locals.

As the SAS commander set up his command post on the east side of Clady and dispatched CRTs into the town and to areas well north and south of it, he prepared to monitor their sweeps. Should any of these teams see or hear anything unusual, they were to fire a red star cluster to signal a response by the remaining team members.

Through the early morning hours and into the late afternoon, his men saw nothing unusual. The locals offered only sullen indifference and an occasional Gaelic insult to these perceived foreigners.

One team, consisting of David Bottomley, Cedric Harrington, and Sergeant Andrew Percy, dropped their packs by the side of the elevated road overlooking the River Finn. The men had patrolled all day and came up empty handed. Instinctively, they began to lower their guards. Bottomley and Harrington sat down and leaned against the bank abutting the road. Percy remained on his feet, and looked about but served little notice to the imposing shadows forming about them. Boredom crept into their minds. They had to patrol two more days and nights before they could head back to Strabane and have a pint or two. Little did they know that the tip on IRA activities around Clady was nothing more than a ruse.

As weary and unconcerned as they felt, their camouflaged and well-hidden assassin intently awaited his opportunity.

Sergeant Percy paced impatiently for a moment as the gunman quietly whispered "Hold still...you bloody bastard." Ned O'Shea then lightly exhaled. The range, carefully marked at 300 meters, gave him no concern. He had practiced at this distance for months. Secluded stretches of Donegal beaches made such opportunities unlimited. Time and again, he'd taken his American made M-1D Garand rifle to the beaches and fired round after round until the weapon became a part of him. He knew it. He and the weapon were one.

O'Shea was the best marksman the IRA had. His 23 confirmed kills of Ulster Defense Association members attested to his proficiency.

He preferred to work alone and didn't care for the loose and sometimes ill-defined control exercised by his immediate superiors. They soon learned that he performed best when given an exact target and left unaccompanied to finish it.

He favored the M-1 Garand to the Lee-Enfield, Britain's service rifle in two world wars. IRA armorers had offered him the Enfield because M-1s were hard to come by. They stressed the Enfield's relatively high rate of fire for a bolt action rifle: The rifle didn't cock when the shooter ejected a spent cartridge. This allowed a relatively inexperienced rifleman to keep his face on the stock when extracting a round. The rifle cocked itself on the forward motion of the bolt. But Ned knew the M-1 had a higher rate of fire and superior ballistics than did the Enfield. Its semi-automatic configuration allowed a marksman to fire each time he pulled the trigger.

Also, accuracy meant more to O'Shea, and the Enfield's relatively low muzzle velocity of 2,400 feet per second made him uncomfortable. He knew his business of human targets and insisted on the .30 caliber M-1 Garand.

As the cross hairs of his scope fixed on Sergeant Andrew Percy's face, Ned O'Shea slowly exhaled. He waited for his entire system to pause. At this range, any slight movement could make him miss. Carefully and deliberately, he took up the trigger slack and then applied slight pressure on the trigger.

Exploding at 2,900 feet per second, the 150 grain soft point bullet tore from the Garand's muzzle. And for an instant, the SAS trooper remained upright. The bullet struck him below his left eye, quickly expanded into its familiar mushroom shape and exited at an upward angle from the back of his head. He collapsed backward onto the bone and brain fragments which preceded him to the ground.

As the rifle recoiled against Ned's shoulder, its bolt instantaneously stripped another round from the eight round clip and drove it into the weapon's chamber. At the same time, Ned turned his sights on a new target—Cedric Harrington.

Harrington had heard the rifle's prior report and felt Sergeant Percy's blood and soft tissues strike his face. He started to rise in terror, but before he could grab his weapon and get to his feet, Ned O'Shea had cranked off another round. It struck the young man in the neck, killing him instantly. He pitched forward in a crumpled mass.

David Bottomley by now had assumed a prone firing position. He saw the muzzle flash west across the river and, much like a hunter startled by a covey of quail, he commenced to fire in a frenzied manner. His failure to take proper aim cost him.

Ready to fire again, Ned squeezed off another round. The bullet struck Bottomley's head, expanded and blended his brains.

O'Shea felt exuberance for himself and his cause—nothing for his victims. He hated the English passionately and would go to any extreme to drive them from his country.

He saw through the scope that Sergeant Percy lay motionless in a grotesque manner. Neither Harrington nor Bottomley moved either, and like Percy, O'Shea instinctively knew they were dead.

He rose, somewhat stiff, from his position behind a grouping of small boulders. He turned to the west and began to run. He wanted to leave his rifle, but he felt naked without it. His thoughts were not on the men he'd just killed, but rather escape.

Seamus Fitzgerald had attempted a similar act two weeks ago, closer to Derry, and met with disaster. He not only missed his target but failed to get away. IRA informants last saw SAS men place him in a van, hands tied behind his back. The morning papers said he died of wounds trying to escape.

O'Shea, however, meticulously planned his escape route. Through a series of maneuvers, he would work his way west and north to a remote cove off Arranmore Island. There he would make for the island in a boat left by IRA operatives. The direct distance was about 65 kilometers, but his route would make it longer, probably two days traveling time.

It wasn't long before O'Shea confronted thick underbrush, resembling an unkempt hedgerow. Moving south along it, he reached a low wooden stake, which marked passage through the thicket. He removed the stake and shoved it into the overgrowth, then pushed aside a cut bush he'd placed there the previous day. Before him lay a narrow path, about 30 inches high. Moving quickly on his hands and knees, he scurried through the undergrowth and emerged 50 meters on the other side.

Ned saw a red star cluster burst to his northeast and sensed the British had rapidly responded to the ambush. He predicted this and wanted to distance himself from the scene. He picked up the pace and ran 800 meters west to an abandoned cottage perched beside some rock outcroppings. The former occupants had deserted the building 20 years before, and its crumbling appearance showed the ravages of both weather and time.

The IRA used this and similar houses as way points in its prosecution of the war on Northern Ireland's western border. Authorities in the Republic seldom checked them.

Ned's concern was to hurriedly vacate the area. He suspected the SAS would alert Irish authorities in the south, and they would begin looking for him.

When he entered the building, he went directly to the fireplace and stopped. Opening the latch on the M-1's butt plate, he removed a cleaning rod and lubricants. He quickly cleansed the barrel and then put a light coat of oil on the rifle. He didn't have time to detail strip the weapon for a thorough cleaning. Instead, he inserted the rifle into a cloth case and eased it into the chimney, cautiously placing it on a hidden shelf.

Famished, he took a can of sardines from the small pack he wore around his waist, but he hardly had time to enjoy the fish. He opened a bottle of fruit juice too and drank it as quickly as he gulped down the sardines. He then shoved both empty containers in his pack so as not to mark his presence. Ned rolled his bicycle out the entrance to the cottage and followed a disappearing path to a secondary road. The route would take him westward toward the Malinmore Head Peninsula.

It was now early evening, and heavy dark clouds were moving eastward from the sea. A chilly spring wind accompanied them, and Ned sensed slight panic as the wind's velocity checked his progress. He knew people on both sides of the border were looking for him.

Soon it began to rain, first as a mist and then very hard. In no time the torrent soaked him. The weather, he realized, would prevent an aerial search; therefore, he eased back on his cycling efforts and continued his push westward.

His original intentions were to turn south to Donegal. Once he'd hit the major road leading there, he would catch a bus north the next day and execute his plan to reach Arranmore Island.

His ambivalence about the weather made him decide otherwise. Although miserable, he followed the secondary roads west and north, taking as direct a route as possible to the boat. Because the rain and growing darkness would better shield his movement, they took priority over his physical comforts.

The 65 kilometers that Ned covered the rest of the night seemed to never end. The rain continued and as night fell, it became difficult to navigate his route. More than once, he checked his wrist compass to right his course, yet he continued like a man possessed.

Around midnight he saw lights. Ned also heard the unmistakable sound of distant waves. He stopped his bicycle at a crossroads and placed it against a stone wall. He crouched beside it and removed a road map and a small flashlight from his pack. He leaned over the map to protect it from the rain and gathered his bearings. He found himself midway between the towns of Maas and Dungloe.

He put the map and flashlight back into his pack and kept moving. Soon he reached the main road between the two towns and turned north. He pushed on past Dungloe, and, although tempted to stop at a local pub for a pint, he forced himself to keep going.

He passed Burtonporte and then made a final turn west. He came upon a deserted cliff overlooking the Atlantic and without hesitation, dismounted his bicycle and pushed it over.

Ned knew a truly tough part of his journey remained. First he had to find the curragh and then push off into the darkness for the island.

Descending a steep slope further to the north, he finally reached the beach. Ned quickly walked 300 meters north and found his vessel right where Padraig Hannaway said it would be.

The curragh, a somewhat light and fragile boat, has been a traditional part of Ireland since the ancient Celtic times. Its basket-like frame and hide covering make it amazingly agile on the high seas. The pointed bow and shallow draft allow it to skim over the waves with considerable ease.

Ned flipped the curragh over and pointed it toward the sea. He then placed the oars inside and pushed it into the surf.

After an initial scare in the churning seas, he soon found the proper cadence and propelled himself toward Arranmore. There he hoped to find dry clothes, food, drink...and safety.

CHAPTER 3

The curragh floated onto the eastern Arranmore beach with ease. Ned jumped into the ankle deep water, pulled the light craft above the water line, and headed inland.

Five-hundred meters to the south and west of his landing point, he heard the metallic sound of someone chambering a rifle round. "Tis I, Ned O'Shea," he yelled in a startled voice.

A flashlight's piercing beam hit his eyes. Instinctively, he raised his forearm to his face and repeated his presence.

"Cead failte, A Ned," a calm, almost melodic voice extended the hundred welcomes to the exhausted IRA soldier.

Ned stood silent for a moment. He digested the Irishman's words and then extended his hand.

"Thomas Larkin, I trust?" asked O'Shea.

"Aye, tis I Ned."

Their awkward introduction complete, Thomas suggested Ned follow him to their quarters. He knew of Ned's plans but hadn't expected him so soon.

As they moved along in the dark, Ned had trouble getting a fix on his welcomer. He watched the shrouded Larkin walk with jerky steps, head up and with apparent conviction. He said nothing.

The two men trekked about 300 meters further south, where they came upon an abandoned monastery.

Thomas took Ned to one of the monastic cells and bid him to get out of his wet clothes and put on the robe hanging behind the door. While Ned was changing, he said he would bring some refreshments.

Ned relaxed for the first time in more than 48 hours. His ordeal extracted a toll; fatigue had set in and he was wet and cold. He removed his clothes and took a quick sponge bath using the basin and pitcher Thomas had put in the room. He dried with the towel placed next to the basin, slipped on the warm robe and pulled slippers onto his feet.

He looked into the small mirror above the washstand and recoiled at his grizzly image. The bright blue eyes which highlighted his square face appeared tired and bloodshot. His thick black hair went in all directions and his four-day old beard told of his recent trials. His light complexion contrasted sharply to his black hair.

Ned's 70 inch frame carried 200 well-distributed pounds and cast an imposing presence. He resembled a fireplug or a bulldog. Yet, he was a quiet, unassuming man who conversed in a careful and deliberate manner. His deep, resonant voice and sharp intellect commanded attention whenever he spoke. Ned O'Shea was a natural leader.

The simple cell he now occupied had a roughly hewn wooden bed with a straw mattress. An equally simple table and chair set below the window. The lone candle on the table provided the only source of light. A crucifix, above the bed, completed the austere furnishings.

As Ned was about to sit on the bed, Thomas Larkin returned with a bag containing a partial loaf of soda bread, several bottles of Guinness stout and a set of dry clothes.

Larkin represented the physical antithesis of O'Shea. He stood 66 inches tall and barely weighed 120 pounds. He had no hair, and his deep brown eyes gave evidence of being dark Irish: a descendant of the Spanish Armada crews which wrecked on the west coast of Ireland.

He had a flippant, peppy voice and a high energy level. Ned wasn't sure if Thomas was like this all the time, or if he was just overjoyed by having someone else on the island.

He smiled readily, only to display a mouthful of decayed and missing teeth.

Aged beyond his 65 years, Thomas Larkin's hunched, arthritic body and bowed legs mocked the tweed jacket and baggy trousers he wore.

His hands were those of a fisherman, all beaten up by years of hard manual labor. And his flushed face, bulbous nose and swollen abdomen showed the ravages of alcohol abuse.

He resembled a freak of nature, and how he could still ambulate seemed a mystery.

But Larkin had zest and direction. And he housed viciousness beneath his charming way.

Well-read on current affairs and an ardent patriot, he had purpose in all that he did, and he feared no one.

"I'm tired Ned, so I'll take me leave. You relax and I'll see you whenever you awake." Thomas smiled and left without saying another word.

Ned stood transfixed for a moment but then decided first things first: He downed three bottles of the stout. This only intensified his hunger. He'd had little nourishment in the past 24 hours.

Ned slowly felt an intense sense of euphoria. Everything had worked out right. He had the satisfaction of his earlier kills; his successful escape; dry, warm clothing...and his fatigue now harbored in safety.

He ate the bread and climbed into the hard but warm bed...and fell asleep immediately.

Ned did not dream or move. His body demanded complete rejuvenation.

The hours drifted by, and he eventually awoke to the muffled sound of waves crashing on the nearby beach. A high pressure system had pushed the rain clouds from the land, and brilliant sunlight filled his Spartan room.

Ned rolled on his back and gazed at the shadows dancing on the ceiling as a strong wind rustled the scraggly shrubs in front of his window. He reflected on yesterday's mission and the primitive satisfaction all successful hunters know. Ned felt invincible in his total preoccupation with the IRA and its cause. It was his reason for existence. Its members were his comrades in arms because Ireland was truly still at war with the British. He felt no remorse for his actions—only for his ancestors dangling from British gallows.

Ned considered the plight of his Ulster acquaintances that, unlike him, had no purpose. Stuck in some nondescript job or floating from one temporary, meaningless position to another, they remained in the subjugated state the English had placed their kind centuries before. They moved like tired zombies and found solace only in drink. They had no confidence or pride. The English had systematically robbed them of all that when they took their land, their language, and their culture. No longer a free people, they'd become the object of condescending ridicule. When in vogue, the world told Polish jokes, but in England they told Irish jokes.

Ned hated the English—a hatred so intense it bordered on the insane. He'd been brought up on an anti-British diet and knew how and why his people had suffered at the hands of their English conquerors.

Fully awake and riled by his reflections on Anglo/Irish history, the young man quickly left his bed, walked to the window and breathed in the clean fresh air.

The ancient and now abandoned monastery, where he'd found temporary respite, stood as a voiceless reminder of the Ireland's monastic glories.

The monks had left centuries before, but somehow Ned felt their presence and imagined their Gregorian chant resonating from the now silent sanctuary.

Gone were their libraries and other priceless contributions of art and literature they had bestowed upon an ignorant and barbaric world.

He walked outdoors and surveyed the grounds, marveling at the structure before him. In recent years, the government had developed the monastery into a youth hostel, but eventually abandoned that effort. Dormant and awaiting a new purpose, Thomas Larkin remained as its caretaker, living alone in the cloistered setting.

Little did the Irish government know that Thomas coordinated the IRA's planning conferences and provided its Ulster officers a safe and appropriate setting for their strategy sessions.

Ned didn't know this; he'd only been directed to be on the island the day following his most recent action.

The secretive operating procedures of the IRA stemmed from its early days when they fought the Black and Tans in Ireland's civil war. Too often, they'd been deceived by what they thought were their own. Time and again, IRA Flying Columns came up short because of a double-cross.

It cost lives, but it taught them to establish cells and tightly control their operations. Like with Ned, he'd only been told where to be but received no other information. He trusted his superiors and never asked questions. He only executed on their directives.

"Ned, did you sleep well, lad?" came the inquiring voice of Thomas Larkin.

The young man turned to see the smiling, ruddy face of his host. He wore a wool fisherman's sweater and the same tweed sport coat and baggy trousers he'd had on the night before. Ned had to bite his lip because the diminutive Larkin projected a clownish appearance. His shapeless, cast-off tweed cap and worn boots made it look like he'd dressed in the dark, but the old man exuded a warmth and friendliness that Ned knew to be genuine.

"I had a good night Thomas, thanks to you. The stout, bread and the warm bed really put me out. I slept 10 hours and feel ready for whatever is next...after maybe a cup of coffee."

Thomas Larkin continued to smile. "Ned, we'll go over to the refectory and have some coffee, soda bread and jam. Our guests should be arriving later this afternoon. Tonight we have an important meeting.

"You've built quite a reputation, and I think headquarters feels tis time to use your talents for something other than picking off Royal Ulster Constabulary blokes or the occasional Tommy. By the way, I heard on a newscast this morning about the SAS men you killed yesterday. Authorities say they have no suspects, but of course believe the IRA had a hand in the affair—brilliant deduction!"

The two men walked to the refectory and entered the time honored hall, and took seats at one of the massive oak tables.

A steaming pot of hot coffee rested at one end, together with generous portions of bread and condiments.

Thomas poured coffee into two mugs and wrapped his hands around the one nearest him; he welcomed its warmth. The refectory had no heat and the sun didn't take the chill off the cavernous interior.

Ned's eyes searched the monks' refectory, marveling at the strength and charm of its architecture. The open beamed ceiling and artfully sculpted stone walls reinforced the beauty of large stained glass windows surrounding the room. Marble statues of saints seemingly stood watch about the chamber.

The bright sunlight sent multicolored rays into all parts of the refectory as Ned continued to be in awe at its rustic beauty.

"You seem to like this place Ned," Thomas observed. "Not everyone shows the interest you do. What is it that catches your eye?"

"I'm not sure Thomas. I studied some art history at university; maybe it helps me put all this into perspective. I marvel at the monks who lived here and built this monastery. They must have been happy men because this place is so beautiful. Unhappy people don't produce things of beauty," the young man responded, still staring at the intricate structure.

"What else did you study Ned?" Larkin continued.

"European history—I wanted to be a teacher. I also studied the usual core requirements the Jesuits demand— plenty of philosophy, languages, literature and science.

They taught me to think and realize not everyone had the inside track on the right answer."

Thomas Larkin, an argumentative type when he wanted to be, challenged Ned. "How do you reconcile what you're doing in the IRA with all the killing?"

"You mean, does it bother my conscience?" O'Shea coolly asked.

"Not necessarily, Ned. I just wondered if you ever had to justify in your mind what you've done the past year," Larkin questioned as he sipped his coffee. "After all, you have disposed of quite a few."

"I thought about it, Thomas," Ned shot back. "I thought about it particularly before I joined the IRA. Ireland's history and the Thomistic treatise on a just war convinced me that the IRA is the only real hope the Irish people have.

"Thomas, the English took our land and until they give it back, there can be no peace.

"And anyone who, to this day, is willing to accept the status quo is no Irishman. We, as a people, must fight until the English tire of the whole mess and leave. Why they don't have the sense General De Gaulle had in Algeria is beyond me. He was wise enough to see France could not win. The Algerian people wanted their independence and freedom. Nothing else would placate them. So, much to the consternation of many Frenchmen, he pulled out and gave them their country. All has been fine since."

"But Ned, this isn't Algeria," Thomas interrupted. But O'Shea continued.

"Listen Thomas, I know all about the settlers in the north and their so-called loyalty to the crown, but by absorption or outright invasion, the English took our land."

Larkin kept it going: "But Thomistic philosophy says there must be a reasonable assurance of victory. We're outnumbered in Ulster and the Republic doesn't back us, nor do the majority of Irishmen north and south."

"Thomas, you know well the Easter Rebellion in 1916 had little support from the Irish people—but look at the results! Everyone finally came around and backed the IRA, and we won our freedom. What we're doing now is just a continuation of that. The Prussian staff officer Clausewitz, before he died in 1831, clarified this concept in his writings. He spoke of war as a form of politics and that it can take several courses. His War of Annihilation doesn't fit us. We can neither mobilize nor militarily defeat the British; therefore, we must engage them in what he called a War of Attrition. We'll whittle away at them, be a constant irritant, frustrate them, exhaust their resources and finally make them simply conclude that it isn't worth it any longer. Our war is a civil war, Thomas, and tis legitimate."

Ned continued, delivering the conclusions he'd accepted in his search of a right cause. "The English won't win, Thomas, because they do not hate us.

They are indifferent to us. The Algerians hated the French and the French couldn't relate to them, so De Gaulle just pulled out and let them alone.

"The French had a similar experience in Vietnam, only they fought it out.

The nation didn't care about what happened to their Legionnaires. In the end, they abandoned them because they too had no hate for the enemy. Vietnam was too far away, and they'd lost interest in their former colony. The battle at Dien Bien Phu finished the French and brought the Viet Minh's hatred to fruition.

"Recent history is replete with such examples. No matter how long it takes, we've got to stay the course because in the end we will win—we will have a united Ireland."

Thomas Larkin looked at his guest with admiration. "You are a good man, Ned. I wish I was your age and had your stamina. Me best years have passed. I still believe in the cause and am a proud IRA member, but me arthritis has hobbled me. You young lads have to keep the fight going. I'm reassured that the likes of you are replacing the old guard." He then lowered his head, resigned that he was no longer an active player.

The two sat in silence for several minutes, then Ned excused himself.

He spent the remainder of the day touring the monastery and walking the beaches. Ned enjoyed others, but he liked being by himself and wondered if he could have lived here as a monk in times past.

Late that afternoon, Thomas Larkin waited on the eastern beach near where he'd intercepted Ned the night before. Soon he saw in the distance a motor launch approaching the island. As the vessel moved closer to the beach, he could make out five men, including the coxswain.

A dock, extending out 10 meters from the beach, provided a stable platform to secure the launch. As it rose and fell with the ground swells, its occupants anticipated their leap onto the dock. All made it easily, except for one. He appeared unsteady and possibly seasick.

After they had jumped, the coxswain reversed the engine and backed away, spun the craft around and headed for the mainland.

The four men and Thomas Larkin exchanged courtesies and headed for the monastery. "I'll show you to your rooms and then we'll meet in the refectory in 45 minutes. I've had a stew simmering all afternoon. It should be rather tasty after we've had a pint or two."

He left the men at their quarters and painfully walked to the kitchen, his swollen ankles and knees protesting his every step.

CHAPTER 4

Asurrealistic aura cloaked the monastery's refectory as the six men drank and ate. Candles provided the only light, their flickering wicks creating ominous shadows which danced off the walls and the pensive men's hardened faces.

Ned felt ill-at-ease. He knew none of the men personally except for Thomas Larkin and the commander, Neal Creedon. He had heard of Shamus O'Shaughnessy, a brigade commander from Belfast, and Sean McGinty, who handled IRA logistics.

Instinctively, Ned didn't like the indolent-looking McGinty. His crafty eyes, recessed in a bony face, moved selectively from one person to another. The rest of him was shiftless and unkempt; he looked dirty. He wore a garish, diamond studded gold ring on his right hand and a thick gold chain around his neck. Somehow, they didn't belong on the man.

The army's operational head was Timothy Higgins. A man in his late forties, he resembled a boxer. His silver and wavy hair gave a contrasting appearance to the pug nose, swollen eyes and several small scars on his face.

Larkin said Higgins had served with British forces in World War II and had spent five years in prison for IRA activities in the 1950s. O'Shea knew of the prison time but not his war record.

Surprisingly, the men hardly spoke. A tenseness hung over the setting. This seemed odd because the IRA had recorded five kills within the past week, all British soldiers. It was a good period. IRA leaders knew slow attrition wreaks havoc on morale. Provided they could keep the conflict at its current level, they felt the British would eventually lose patience.

Finally, Higgins began to address the group. "Gentlemen, the Irish Republican Army is on the eve of its next major campaign. We've operated in a low intensity environment since the 1956 Troubles, and the situation for our people in Ulster has grown only worse. Mind you, we've got to show the British bastards that we're willing to up the ante and not accept the status quo which they're so anxious to perpetuate. The only way we can open the campaign on a serious note is to strike boldly. We intend to do just that. We intend to capture the whole world's attention for our cause."

The men sat rigid and open-mouthed at what was to follow. Higgins's words and his hard, deep-blue eyes drilling into each of them, set the tone. "Next month, the queen will visit Derry. We intend to assassinate her."

No one spoke.

The extraordinary proposal left them all stunned and without words. One by one they looked at Higgins with guarded fear. But their reservations came to a halt as the IRA commander continued.

"The queen's itinerary has her tightly controlled. She won't mix with the ordinary citizens and will not travel far, but we do have a window of opportunity. She will visit a horse farm east of Derry in the vicinity of Limavady. Apparently the queen wants to upgrade her stables, and she intends to take a serious look at the stock there.

"Security will be tight, but she'll have to walk around and watch the horses go through their paces.

"High ground surrounds the farm out to distances of 1,000 meters. I know it's asking a lot, but a good marksman could hit her, even at that range. He'd have to position himself well in advance and patiently await his chance. It may never come, but we must try."

Ned now knew why he was at the table. They had selected him to do the job. Did he hate the British that much? God, what an assignment!

Higgins continued with the plan. "Ned, Neal Creedon has advised me of your repeated successes this past year. I've had Sean here comb our records of both active and inactive IRA members. We have some proven marksmen, but none of your stature. You're the only one who is competent enough to do this job.

"We've considered many inactive IRA members in the past for such special operations, but they all balked—too many other priorities and responsibilities. Families and jobs make them cautious. Besides, their skills don't measure up to yours. I don't think they could hit the queen at 200 meters; 1,000 would be out of the question.

"Ned, we want to bring you to the region as soon as possible before British security elements start nosing around. You'll be employed as a stable hand and thus have a chance to reconnoiter the farm and see if it's feasible to build a spider trap or whatever else you want to devise. The key is getting into position for the kill. I'm told you like the American .30 caliber Garand. Good choice, but we'll have to special load ammunition for you. At 1,000 meters, you'll need a 200 grain bullet for accuracy.

"McGinty will provide you money to cover your expenses over the next month. You'll initially stay with him in Derry. Shamus's men will give you a definitive briefing of the operating area; then you'll be on your own. Let us know of any logistical requirements you might have, and we'll oblige you.

"I cannot overemphasize the importance of this action. We must make it work. Our credibility and a united Ireland rest on it. Does anyone have questions?"

Thomas Larkin spoke first. "Why the queen? She's a noncombatant."

"So was Adolph Hitler!" Higgins shot back. "Had someone taken him out early in the war, Germany would have been without direction. The spirit, the soul of the National

Socialist's movement had to remain alive, and that wouldn't have been possible without him.

"The English too would suffer a similar fate. And they would be helpless to react. What are they going to do, invade their own territory?"

Larkin, ever the critic, sighed. "Jasus, she's respected around the globe. Killing her would pit the world community against us. Tis almost like killing the pope. The reaction would be wholly negative."

Higgins paused for a moment and cast a troubled look at Larkin. "I'm aware of that Thomas, but when the emotions abate, cooler heads will ask why one would perpetrate such an act. Only then will something constructive happen. In the interim, the English will realize that the cost of holding onto Ulster will be too great."

Ned, having more at stake than anyone, hesitantly threw in, "Suppose I'm able to kill her. How do I escape?"

Higgins, happy to be off the topic of geopolitics, discussed the plan in greater detail. "We're arranging a series of remote controlled diversionary explosions in conjunction with your shot. We'll create as much confusion as possible in and around the area. Chances are they won't know where the shot came from. We have farmers in the region that will hide you. Operatives at the horse farm will orient you to the escape route and give you definitive directions regarding all the particulars. Be assured, we have no intention of letting you swing," Higgins concluded with a sardonic grin.

After a terse pause, Higgins lifted a pint. "Slawncha gus sale agut."

The others subtly echoed the toast...health and wealth to you.

The refectory became silent again. The ominous scheme was for real. The men knew they'd be embarking on a perilous journey with possible catastrophic consequences. But other Irish patriots had gone against terrible odds. These were willing to do the same.

Neither answered.

O'Shaughnessy continued, "What we discussed last night was not some kind of impulsive plan. Both military and political wings of the IRA have pondered it for months. We have considered all of its ramifications. It is simply something we must do. I know it is extreme, but our cause is in peril. We must do more than just passively let the English maintain their hold on our land.

"And, might I add, aside from our group last night, only four other people know of its existence. I trust all of them implicitly. Nothing has been compromised," concluded O'Shaughnessy.

"Aye," said Neal Creedon. "Tis true. Our small element will carry out the act. No one else has specific knowledge of the plan."

Ned looked at the two me and said, "I dah not question your decision. Tis just a heavy burden you have placed on me. And it isn't something that I have taken lightly."

Larkin did not speak, but rose and went to retrieve some soda bread and jam.

Silence surrounded the men once again.

As they sipped their drinks, McGinty came into the refectory. He hadn't shaved, nor did it appear he had washed.

He poured a cup of coffee and dropped onto the bench next to the massive oak table where everyone sat. He lit a cigarette and told everyone how well he'd slept. It didn't seem like anyone cared, because no one said anything.

At that point, there was little food left.

"Our boat is scheduled to arrive shortly. I suggest we gather our things and make for the dock. There will be three cars waiting for us. Neal and Shamus will take one and I the other. Sean, you and Ned will take the third car and drive to your home in Derry. Along the way, I want you and Ned to go over whatever logistical requirements he will have. Within a couple of days, Neal will contact you to find where you're billeted, Ned. He will stay put until we have everything in place and it's safe to move him to the farm," O'Shaughnessy explained. It was 8:00 A.M.

The men rose from the table and left the refectory. Larkin gathered the cups and plates and took them to the kitchen. Soon, all of them, as if on cue, gathered on the dock. In the distance they could see the motor launch which had brought them to the island the day before. The coxswain kept the craft headed into the wind. As he approached the dock, he throttled back and eased the boat alongside it.

As it pitched in the swirling surf, Creedon, O'Shaughnessy and McGinty gingerly eased themselves into the boat. Ned turned and looked at Larkin before he joined them.

"Thank you for your kindness and concern, Thomas. I will not forget them," Ned said as he put out his hand.

Larkin grasped it with both of his and shook it warmly. His eyes, full of anxiety, conveyed a message stronger than any words he could have spoken.

He let go of Ned's hand and watched as the young IRA man climbed into the boat and disappeared into the distance.

Larkin turned and sadly walked back alone to the monastery.

The boat, meanwhile, was on a 130 degree course towards Dungloe where the IRA operatives would pick up their cars. As they weaved around the various small islands leading into the bay west of town, the men said nothing. All had the same agenda on their minds, except for Sean McGinty. Duplicity marked his thoughts.

The coxswain approached the Dungloe beach in the same competent manner he'd docked at Arranmore. He throttled back and let the waves lift the sturdy craft onto the beach. The men jumped out and pulled the boat above the water line. The coxswain joined them as they walked up to the town. McGinty paid him 35 pounds as they parted company near the rented automobiles.

The four men strolled to the cars. McGinty gave them their keys, and they exchanged farewells. O'Shaughnessy advised them before departing that he would arrange for another planning session at an undisclosed location in or around Derry within two weeks. By then, he hoped McGinty would have cared for Ned's logistical needs: lodging, weapon, ammunition, money, fake identification and passport.

McGinty assured him that he would take care of it.

O'Shaughnessy took a serpentine route back to Belfast. He went south and east, staying in the Irish Republic the whole time until he reached Dundalk on the east coast. He turned north there and passed safely into Northern Ireland and on to Belfast without incident.

Neal Creedon intersected at Strabane, a bit north of Clady where Ned had made his kills. He wasn't as fortunate. The border crossing was heavily guarded, and the police searched each vehicle entering and exiting while questioning the occupants.

When Creedon told them he lived in Derry, they wondered what he was doing in the Irish Republic. He told them he was on holiday visiting relatives in Sligo. He sensed they didn't believe him, but they found nothing suspicious on him or in the car, so they let him pass.

Creedon was uncomfortable with the heightened security and felt ill-at-ease about the upcoming plan to execute the queen. He drove on to his humble home in Bogside, outside the walls of Derry. It was in the sight of the column and statue immortalizing the Reverend George Walker, Major of Derry during the 1689 siege.

The Catholics in the present day region were never welcomed inside the city walls, and were forced to settle in the bog lands outside them. Each morning they awoke to look up and see the statue. Years later, Creedon would have the satisfaction of blowing up the insult. Everyone in Bogside laughed and cheered when it happened.

O'Shea and McGinty took a more direct route to Derry, through the historic regions of Lough Swilly and south of Rathmullen.

As they drove to Derry, they talked little. Ned wasn't sure why this IRA logistician appeared reticent to address any topics.

Finally, Ned spoke directly to the man behind the wheel. He told McGinty that he needed his rifle to kill the queen. No other weapons would be acceptable. He had his Garand sighted in and would not have the time or opportunity to do the same with another rifle.

McGinty looked over at him. The cigarette, loosely hanging from his lips, reinforced the apparent indifference the man had for Ned's concern.

"Sean, I'm serious. I need the rifle."

"Where is it?" McGinty asked.

Ned proceeded to tell him that the rifle was located in the abandoned cottage south and west of Clady. The structure had the code name *trinket*, for which IRA headquarters had map coordinates. It would be a simple case of directing an operative in Clady to retrieve the weapon, disassemble it, and transport it to the site of the ambush.

"I'll see that this is done," said McGinty, still conveying no enthusiasm or interest.

They continued to drive east. Ned decided to engage the laconic McGinty in topics other than the IRA. Maybe his reservations about him were off the mark, but he still intuitively felt uncomfortable about the man.

"Do you have a family, Sean?"

McGinty's eyes became shifty again, and he squinted at Ned.

"Why?" he asked.

"Sean, I'm trying to make conversation. We're to work together, and I want to establish a positive rapport with you. How you do your job determines whether I'm successful. You seem secretive. That's all right, but there needs to be some sense of trust between us. I don't feel that right now. There's a lot hanging on this operation, and I need a sense of assurance. I need confidence about those with whom I'm working."

McGinty gave a petulant shrug of his shoulders, glared at O'Shea, and then shifted his eyes back to the road.

"I don't really grasp much about you either, O'Shea. And I'm not sure I want to. I know how to make this thing work logistically. Headquarters didn't give me the job because I'm irresponsible. They gave it to me because of my organizational skills and my ability to see a job through to completion.

"Two years ago the Rigney furniture company, the largest in the region, promoted me to warehouse manager. I oversee fifteen men and hold a large and valuable inventory. I coordinate all their shipping, receiving and deliveries. It's demanding, but I'm good, and they know it.

"Rigney has their main office in London. They are a big British company and pretty tight—kind of like family. For that reason, tis out of the ordinary that they would pick me—an outsider so to speak. None of them knew if I was a practicing Catholic, loyal to the crown or what. What they did know was that I showed the most potential, worked hard, fed them good ideas, and kept me mouth shut. No one knew much about me outside of work, and that is what gave me the opportunity to rise in the company. I produce and keep me mouth shut! Some of the Presbyterian bastards under me tried to raise hell because management selected me over them. They are so inbred that an outsider isn't to be trusted. But I wouldn't stoop to their level, and pretty soon things were all right. Everyone now sees me as loyal and competent.

"I've made it! I'm not one of those unemployed Bogside bastards who has screwed himself out of a place at the table. No, I've got pride; I've got money, and I've got stature! And I don't live in some dump.

"And because I appear content, dedicated to my job, and an asset to the company, no one suspects me association with the IRA," McGinty concluded.

O'Shea sat silent for a time. He tried to compute exactly where McGinty was coming from. He concluded that the warehouse foreman had purposely cloaked himself in an air of uncertainty, and that ambition consumed him.

Ned worried. Did McGinty have a greedy flaw in his character? His pejorative observations about his less fortunate Bogside acquaintances disturbed Ned. McGinty looked down on them and had no empathy for their plight. Selflessness was lacking, and Ned brooded about Sean's commitment to the IRA.

The two men rolled on past Letterkenny, the last major town in the Irish Republic, and soon could see Derry in the distance. They crossed the border into Northern Ireland without incident.

"O'Shea, you will stay at me house tonight. By tomorrow, I'll have made arrangements for you to lodge elsewhere. You'll remain in a covert status until we take care of your identification papers and passport. At the earliest opportunity, we'll move you to the horse farm, and you can start your job.

"Why the passport, Sean?"

"If something goes wrong in a big way, we may have to conduct you out of the country, and I do mean completely off the island. I hope it doesn't come to that, but we've had to do it in the past. We have one lad freezing his butt off in Canada. Another we sent to the States four years ago. The bastard recently informed us he isn't coming back.

"Another thing while I'm thinking of it: me wife has no knowledge of me IRA activities. Make no mention or inference about anything to do with the organization. We'll make like I've been on an overnight delivery job to Armagh, and you have returned with me to shop for some additional office furniture. She is not Catholic. She comes from a long line of Scots who can trace their ancestry back to the early settlements on the Ards Peninsula," said McGinty.

O'Shea cringed when he heard this. He felt even more uncomfortable about McGinty now. Nothing made sense. How could he be in such an important position with the upper echelons of the IRA and have such a suspicious background?

They reached Derry, and McGinty drove his car to the upper middle class neighborhood and parked in front of a duplex. As the two men exited the car, McGinty's wife and daughters stood on the porch with pleasant smiles on their faces.

McGinty climbed the stairs, kissed his wife and hugged his two daughters. The affection was genuine, yet reserved.

"Martha, this is Tim Cosgrove. He's with the company in Armargh that we made the delivery to yesterday. He'll visit our showrooms tomorrow and then head home. I told him he could stay with us tonight," said McGinty.

"Hello Tim...welcome to our home.

"These are our daughters, Kate and Karen. Can you say hello to Mr. Cosgrove, girls?" said McGinty's wife.

Ned smiled and shook hands politely with the three, and followed them inside.

It was larger than most homes he had been in. It was artfully decorated with furniture and draperies that he figured McGinty bought at cost. Lladros graced the tables. Original oil paintings hung on the walls. Martha had family pictures on the sideboard: Sean, their children and her relatives.

Martha McGinty had a formal air about her. She smiled readily, like she practiced it. Her teeth were perfect, and so was her figure. She was poised. Ned wondered if she had attended a finishing or modeling school because of her cosmopolitan aura.

She stood sixty-seven inches tall, was in her early thirties, had flaxen hair, blue eyes and a narrow face—a very attractive woman. She moved gracefully and exuded a distinctive feminine charm. She knew she had class. It welled up in her unspoken self-confidence. And she looked clean and well-groomed, unlike her husband.

Was she the cause of Sean's boundless ambition? Did he have to satisfy her need for stature and comfort? Somehow the two didn't fit. Sean was coarse, lacked social skills, and was anything but handsome. How did they ever meet, and why did they marry?

Ned missed being alone. He already felt uncomfortable because things weren't adding up. He sensed he was in an enemy environment.

"Do you have any children, Mr. Cosgrove?" Karen asked.

"No, I don't, Karen. I'm not married."

"That's sad. My grandmother says that children are a great joy."

"I'm sure they are, Karen. Maybe one day I will have some."

Martha broke in. "Enough of the questions, Karen. Let's let daddy and Mr. Cosgrove clean up for supper. Tim, you'll stay in the guest room over there. Towels are on the bed. The bath is the next door over. We'll eat in about thirty minutes."

McGinty had already gone to the refrigerator and opened a beer. He gulped it down and then began to slowly pick his nose.

"Sean, do you think Tim would like a beer too?" Martha asked.

"Never thought of it," he answered. "Want one there, Mr. Cosgrove?"

"I don't think so...maybe later," Ned replied.

Ned turned and went into the guest room and closed the door. He sat on the bed and mused. He could hear Martha dressing down Sean. She called him rude and crude. Tomorrow couldn't come soon enough. He thought he wanted out of the house and away from McGinty.

Thirty minutes later Ned heard a timid knock on the door. He opened it and Karen stood looking up at him. "We are ready to eat, sir."

Ned smiled at the little girl. He thought of the joy she mentioned earlier about having children. He felt unfulfilled.

The meal Martha prepared was superb. Unlike the hardy, but unadorned offerings that Thomas Larkin presented, this one was succulent. Ned's place setting had English bone china and sterling silverware. The water and wine glasses were Waterford crystal. The napkin represented the finest in Irish lace. He felt underdressed for the formal surroundings.

No one prayed or said anything before the meal. Sean just commenced to pass the bowls and the platter around and everyone helped themselves.

The girls mirrored their mother. Although the younger one struggled a bit with the silver, which was too big for her hands, they nevertheless ate gracefully.

"Tis a superb meal, Mrs. McGinty. After a day on the road, it truly warms me innards, and I thank you very much. You are most hospitable," said Ned.

"You are very welcome, Tim."

Martha smiled liberally at the compliment, as if she seldom received any.

Her husband gulped down his food, as he did earlier with his beer. He was preoccupied and said little. After eating, he excused himself, saying, "I have some administrative things I must finish before tomorrow, so I'll take me leave. I imagine it will be close to midnight before I'm back. Don't wait up for me."

As McGinty rose and left the table, he acknowledged neither his wife nor his daughters. He just went out the door. It was an awkward moment.

Once he was gone, Martha shifted gears. She acted as though some constraining presence was lifted, and she smiled even more. She began to chat and appeared to enjoy Ned's presence.

Without direction from their mother, the two girls cleared the table. They then excused themselves and went to their room.

"Your daughters impress me, Mrs. McGinty. They are real ladies. You have brought them up well. They are a credit to you and your husband."

"Thank you, Tim. That is kind of you to say."

Martha lifted her wine glass and sipped the fine Gamay Beaujolais she had served with her meal.

"Tim, you seem quiet and absorbed like Sean. Are many men like that? I ask because my father was the same way.

He worked hard and didn't share his feelings with any of us.

"Sean works hard, too. In fact I worry about him at times because he puts in so many hours. But it paid off. He received a nice promotion and a raise not long ago, and we are very proud of him."

"I'm happy for all of you. I have noticed he's very efficient. I am not surprised that he has done well," Ned offered politely.

He couldn't be sure if Martha was mouthing the party line as the faithful wife, or if she really meant it. He sought to change the subject.

"Mrs. McGinty, please don't take this as me being too inquisitive, but you appear to be an educated woman. Can I ask where you studied?"

"Not at all," as she flashed another smile, this one even more genuine.

"My parents sent me to study music at a conservatory in Glasgow. Daddy became very ill in my third year and died before I could complete my studies. I never went back. Our family went through some difficult times after his death. Mommy never really got over his passing, and we fell on financial hard times. I went to work as a secretary, and my musical skills declined and all but vanished.

"I met Sean shortly after I started working, and we married within the year. The rest is sort of history. We have two daughters and a nice home. We are fortunate."

She didn't say she was happy, and this bothered Ned. Yet he had no point of reference in judging couples. He was an orphan and had only known the influence of the good nuns in his impressionable years. The concept of a real family was foreign to him. He often wondered about having a real mother and father…and siblings, too. He wanted to have a family like Sean, yet he was unsure of his ability to commit.

"Would you like another glass of wine, Tim?"

"Aye. Tis a good vintage."

She went to the kitchen, brought back the bottle, and poured the wine into Ned's glass. Only a little remained, and Martha put that in her glass.

"Do you like politics, Tim?"

Puzzled by her question, Ned offered a bland reply. "I am indifferent to it. I concentrate on me work and don't give much thought to the subject."

"Sean is the same way, Tim. I try and engage him in conversations about the problems that face the community here in Derry, but he just grunts. He'd rather wager on the bloody horse races."

"I suppose tis a diversion from his work. We all need such things," said Ned.

"I know, Tim, but at least he could offer an opinion. What about you? Do you have an opinion about our troubles here in Derry?" she asked, her eyes bulging and the inflection of her voice signaling hostility.

Ned tried again to convey indifference. "I have no opinion about Derry. I do not come here often, and I read little about it."

He wondered if Martha's wine was talking. He'd noticed that Sean drank none, and that she had refilled her glass several times.

"Well, do you have an opinion about the IRA, Tim? Do you believe in a united Ireland?"

"Mrs. McGinty, I subscribe to the belief that one should not argue religion, politics, or women. I really do not care to discuss such topics. I mean that as no offense. I am enjoying the evening very much. I do not want to ruin it by me saying something that might offend you."

"I understand, Tim," she replied softly.

Martha sat back and looked deeply into Ned's eyes. She was a deceptively aggressive woman, despite her social charm.

"Forgive me, Tim. My frustration about not being able to address such topics with Sean got the best of me. Let's talk about you. You're a handsome fellow. I would think a man like you would be married. Do you have a girl?"

"As I said, Mrs. McGinty, I don't talk about women," Ned replied.

"Well, what do you talk about? I fix a nice dinner and try to be a gracious hostess, but for what? My husband gets up and leaves, and his business client sits here like some kind of vegetable!"

Martha's outrage shocked Ned. Before he could say anything, she drank the remainder of her wine and asked him if he'd like a brandy. Without waiting for a reply, she went to the kitchen and took two brandy snifters down, tilted them and poured two perfect glasses.

"Let's sit in the living room," she said.

Ned followed her, still confused at the sudden change in temperament and passivity.

Martha sat in a wing back chair facing the couch. She looked at Ned as he eased into the plush sofa.

She had placed his brandy on the end table next to him.

Before she said anything, her two daughters came out, dressed for bed, and told their mommy good night. She kissed them both. They turned and said good night to Ned too, and skipped to their bedroom and closed the door.

"I am starved for conversation, Tim. My husband has so many things going in his life that we hardly speak anymore. He provides me a good life, materially, but it ends there," she said regretfully. Martha punctuated her remorse by sipping from the brandy glass as strain and anger pocked her face.

Ned took a drink too and tried to prepare himself. For what, he didn't know.

"Martha, I really don't know you very well. I am a bit uncomfortable with you expressing your personal problems with me."

"What's the matter with you—can't handle adult conversation?"

"Yes, Martha, I can handle it."

"What would you do if you had a wife and she didn't talk with you, and she ignored you?" asked Martha.

"Do you nag him?"

"Why do you ask?"

"Possibly he doesn't communicate because you talk down to him."

"You men are insufferable. You have no sense of a woman's needs. You just keep everything in and expect us to act like nothing is wrong.."

She took another drink from her glass and began to cry. She put her head back in the chair and sobbed.

Ned felt helpless as he sat and watched the tortured woman release her emotions. Then suddenly she stopped, as if someone had turned off a valve. She looked at him and smiled, then commenced to speak again.

"Why is there so much hate in Northern Ireland? There is such a chilling atmosphere in our community. No one trusts anyone. Tis as though we have flocks of different birds forced to fly with one another. The need to be with one's own dominates daily life.

"Sean and I are like two different species. He is nominally Catholic, and I am Presbyterian. Other folks look on us with suspicion. Why can't they leave us alone?

"Tell me Tim, what do you think of Presbyterians? I suppose you're Catholic because you're from Armagh," she said.

"I don't know much about Presbyterians…only what I read in Voltaire's 'Letters on the English' which is what he wrote when he took refuge there."

"What did Voltaire say, Tim?"

"He said the Episcopal and Presbyterian sects were the two largest in Great Britain. He said Presbyterianism is the established religion in Scotland, but its ministers were poor compared to the Episcopalians. And they have pretty strict laws about what you can do on Sunday. Only the elite or genteel play on that day. The rest of the folks either go to church, to a tavern or to visit their mistresses. I don't remember much else."

Martha laughed. "So a certain percentage drank and fornicated on the Lord's Day."

"That's what Voltaire said, Martha. Has anything changed?"

Martha laughed again. "I don't know, except that on Sunday I neither go to church, to a tavern nor to bed with Sean.

"I don't think your friend Voltaire had any feel for the Irish problem, about The Troubles here in the north. There isn't much toleration of religion by Protestant or Catholic.

"Religion…if that's what it is, I don't want any part of it," she said and emptied her glass.

Her words lack cadence. She tried to maintain her poise, but her eyes lost their fixating ability. She no longer portrayed the image she presented when Ned first met her.

"I'm sorry for you," he answered as he, too, finished his brandy. "If you will excuse me, I'm a bit tired. Your husband and I have a full day tomorrow. Thank you again for the wonderful meal. I have not eaten that well in a long time. You are a superb cook and a wonderful hostess. Your husband and daughters are indeed fortunate."

She smiled at his kindness as Ned rose, entered his room and closed the door.

He took a toothbrush from the shaving kit Thomas Larkin had given him and went to the bathroom. When he returned to his room, he noticed Martha sitting in the same fixed position in the wing back chair. She had assumed the exclusive smile of a tipsy lady.

Ned undressed and eased under the bed covers. He was tense and disturbed about the bizarre actions of Martha McGinty's demeanor and comments. She displayed the utmost in charm, and then lost it all by the end of the evening. He felt the woman was deeply distressed.

Ned turned to the wall. He was exhausted. The recent ambush, the flight to the monastery, and the unimaginable mission assigned slowly gave way to fitful sleep.

Suddenly he was awakened by the soft touch of a hand on his left shoulder. He froze. The hand moved gently down his arm. He turned to discover Martha McGinty standing over him in a gossamer nightgown, every curve of her body outlined by the light behind her from the open door.

"I just tucked in my daughters and wondered if I might do the same for you, Tim," she whispered.

He was dumbstruck! The electricity of her words left him speechless. Finally, he said, "Leave…leave now!" His voice, low and scathing, overpowered her with its authority. Even in her inebriated state, she caught the full impact of his message. Without hesitation or anger, she left the room. The proposition now intensified his earlier apprehensions—first McGinty, now her. Who can be trusted was an even bigger issue as he tossed and turned. The sleep and rest he so badly needed failed to overtake him.

The next morning, all parties were at the breakfast table at 8:00 A.M. They ate eggs, sausage and biscuits. Like the meal the previous night, it was filling and delectable.

The girls, ready for school, bid their parents goodbye and left giggling as they paid their respects to Ned. He smiled at them and wished them good cheer.

Martha said nothing to either her husband or to Ned. Both had rejected her: one recently, the other by his continued preoccupation and indifference. She remained lonely and incomplete.

The two men left shortly after the girls. Ned ritualistically thanked his hostess for her hospitality. She acknowledged him in the same mechanistic way.

Outside, Ned felt a wave of relief. Initial vibes were anything but good. He doubted McGinty. He considered the man's relationship with his wife absurd. And what was his real commitment to the IRA? That appeared to be on the back burner.

Possibly his intuitive sense had him off target. Maybe he was too harsh in his judgment of McGinty and of his surroundings. Only time would tell.

They climbed into McGinty's car and started for Bogside.

CHAPTER 6

McGinty changed. He spoke succinctly, like a man in control. Gone was his prior reticence.

"I have you a private room loaned to us by Jerry Emmet. He will also make your false identification papers and passport. He works in a print shop near my warehouse. He is solid IRA. Spends much time in the background, but provides what we need when it comes to things like this.

"I suggest you remain in your room until we have your papers and approval from headquarters to relocate to the farm. I have arranged to have your rifle picked up and transported there. The proper ammunition will be there too. And we'll have the right kind of clothing on hand also. The key right now is for you to stay hidden. I suspect we'll have you ready within four days."

Somehow, Ned felt better. McGinty obviously had worked hard after he'd left the table the previous evening. Things were falling into place. His neglected wife was his problem and vice-versa.

McGinty halted the car in front of a dilapidated two story structure on the southwest edge of Bogstown and pointed to an upper level window in the run-down building.

"That is where you will stay. Here is the key to the room. It has a telephone. I caution you to use it only in the case of an emergency. Try never to call my house. I don't want my wife suspecting anything. She feels I'm up to something — like having an affair maybe. That silly twit sounds round-the-bend all too often."

Ned never mentioned her actions the previous night. But he figured McGinty contributed greatly to her emotional trauma. In the right hands, she would be a great wife. Too bad the two of them ended up together.

"Good luck, Ned. I will check on you periodically," said McGinty as he extended his hand.

The two men shook hands as Ned thanked McGinty for everything he had done.

Ned climbed out, closed the door and watched the small Fiat disappear around the corner. He gazed at his surroundings for a moment and made note of the broken window on the first level, then walked inside the crumbling and battered structure. It was terrible. The stairwell smelled musty, and paint was peeling everywhere. The stairs leading up were darkened with dirt.

Ned climbed the stairs and turned left to a door with the number four on it. He inserted the key in the lock and heard it click. He slowly opened the door, afraid of what he might find.

The interior surprised him. The room was clean, freshly painted, and contained some decent furniture. He noted the neatly made twin bed, a desk lamp and telephone, a small dresser, and a lounge chair. There was a bathroom with soap, a toothbrush and a razor. And in the corner was a small refrigerator and table with a hot plate and five-inch television. Above the table were shelves lined with canned goods, dishes and pans.

Things were Spartan, but quite adequate. Ned knew he could remain hidden with no difficulty. He would sit and wait for directions to move.

He opened the refrigerator. It was well stocked for its size, and even included some Harp lager. He smiled. Harp is brewed across the border in Dundalk and his hosts apparently didn't want any British imports desecrating this IRA safe house.

A few books and magazines lay on the dresser. Ned didn't feel like reading at that moment. Instead, he just looked out the window at the appalling appearance of Bogstown. It made him think of the back issues of "Punch," the English sarcastic periodical. The publication struck to the widely held opinions of the Irish. They were crude, backwards, of low intelligence and devoted to drink.

Ned noticed the wall in Derry when he and McGinty drove through town—a presage to the more violent era to follow between Protestants and Catholics. Cryptic artwork and messages called for "No Popery Here," "Keep Ulster Protestant," "No Queen Here," and "Provisionals for Freedom."

He thought of the American poet Robert Frost and his poem "Mending Wall," and how Frost observed "Something there is that does not love a wall…" and "Good fences make good neighbors."

"Would the wall of Northern Ireland ever come down?" he sarcastically murmured to himself.

The afternoon drifted by. Ned had no desire to walk about or explore. He'd had a full plate the past few days, and he wanted time to digest the magnitude of the current undertaking.

Shortly after 5:00 P.M., the phone rang. An unfamiliar yet melodious voice intoned a query.

"Ned, tis Jerry Emmit here. I trust Sean told you about me?"

"He did, Jerry."

"Good, then I will be dropping by in about an hour. We have some administrative things to attend to."

The phone went silent, and Ned slowly hung up the receiver. His respite was short lived.

An hour and twenty minutes later, Jerry Emmit knocked on Ned's door and announced his presence. Ned opened the door and invited the thin man into the room. He carried a small leather bag which he placed on the desk. The two men then shook hands and smiled.

"I shan't be but a few minutes, Ned. Sean probably told you I'm a printer and will arrange for your passport and other false identification papers. We'll give you a driver's license and some other nonsense. Hopefully, you won't have to use any of them, but just in case..."

Jerry Emmit then opened the bag he'd brought in and took out a camera and several envelopes.

"I don't like the idea of having me picture taken, Jerry."

"I understand, Ned, but we need it for the passport."

"What about the film? It worries me about who might have access to the negatives."

"Don't worry. We have a darkroom at work, and I will develop the film meself and take care of the negatives."

"I understand, Jerry. Tis just that I don't like having so many players involved. One weak link and not only am I done for, but the whole plan goes awry. Numbers equate to trouble. I'm sorry; tis just the way I feel."

"I understand, Ned, but there are some you must trust. You can't pull this off by yourself, whatever the IRA has planned."

"You mean you don't know, Jerry?"

"No. I do what I'm told, Ned. The less I know the better. I can always dummy out should the authorities come nosing around."

Ned felt a little relieved.

Jerry Emmet quickly loaded the older 35mm camera and attached a bulb to the flash attachment.

"I'm going to take a few flash pictures and then open up the lens and see if I can capture some without the flash."

He took four flash pictures with Ned standing against a naked wall. He then finished the 12 exposure roll using various lens openings.

"I think we should have a picture or two we can use. That should do it." Emmet rewound the film, took it from the camera and placed it in a mental container. He then took some false documents from the folders and had Ned sign above the fictitious name of Kevin Kinney.

"That should do it, Ned. I'll have everything done by the day after tomorrow and will bring them by. In the meantime, should you need anything, call me."

Jerry handed Ned a card with his telephone number on it.

"Thanks, Jerry. I'm not planning on going anywhere, so I'll be here."

The two men shook hands again, and Jerry Emmet left the room and closed the door behind him. Ned watched from the second story window as he exited the building. He walked quickly onto the adjoining street and disappeared among the row houses of Bogside.

Ned walked to the refrigerator and took out a Harp, opened it, and drank it hastily. He opened another and sat in the lounge chair gazing out the window, thinking of nothing in particular.

The telephone rang and snapped him from his daydream.

"Ned, this is Sean. I wanted to know if you have everything you need and if Jerry Emmet came by?"

"I am fine. Jerry left a short time ago—said he'd be back day after tomorrow with everything."

"Good! Stay put and we'll contact you soonest." Click.

Now it was sit and wait time. Ned was beginning to feel vulnerable and like a prisoner. This part of the plan made him nervous. He was dealing with men he didn't know well, and he kept thinking of Thomas Larkin's admonition about not trusting anyone. He reached into his trouser pocket and fingered the small handgun Thomas had given him. Her removed it and opened the chamber to view the two rounds sitting in the barrels. He removed them and studied their makeup. Both had the distinctive cone shape of hollow points. Deadly at a short range, they would expand and inflict a ghastly wound. His kills had always been at great distances. Would he ever come face to face with an enemy and have to use the Derringer?

Killing had become an indifferent act for Ned. He neither knew nor had met any of his victims. Best that way he figured, but then would any of that change?

He dismissed his thoughts and came back to the current time and place.

So far, everyone had done what they said they would do. Jerry Emmet was no exception He returned at the designated time and delivered the false documents.

Ned looked at them and marveled at their authenticity. Again, he felt reassured and sensed both Jerry and McGinty knew what they were doing.

"These are quite professional looking, Jerry," Ned said.

"Thank you. The wonderful part about me job is that I have access to all types of printing and photo processing equipment, and I know how to use it. I often work overtime and am alone. No one either watches me or suspects I am an IRA operative. I keep to meself. Most think I'm an innocuous bloke, and I want to keep it that way."

"What about the negatives?" asked Ned.

"Sean came by about 9:30 P.M. last night to check on me progress. He took them."

"Why?"

"I don't know. He just said he'd better take them as well as the pictures I didn't use in preparing your papers."

"Is this what you usually do, Jerry?"

"I wouldn't worry, Ned. Sean knows his business."

"That isn't what I asked. Is this what he usually does?"

"I've prepared documents four times before. He took the pictures of two of them."

"Were any of the IRA men lost that you prepared papers for?"

"Two."

"Which two?"

"Come to think of it, the two that Sean retained the negatives of. But I wouldn't jump to any conclusions. I'd trust Sean with me own kin. He is a dedicated soul. That he is."

Jerry Emmet could see the distrust on Ned's face. He was not convincing and had never thought of the picture discrepancy before Ned asked. He didn't want to be involved in any suspicions. A pedestrian kind of man, he just wanted to do what he was told and make some small contribution to the IRA cause.

"I'd better get on, Ned." Jerry said as he took his leave before any more conversation started.

Was this a crack in the dike? Was he overly critical, or was it a legitimate concern? He didn't know, but he felt uncomfortable, and he wanted to discuss it with someone, even McGinty.

He got his chance. Two days later, Sean McGinty knocked on Ned's door. It was early Saturday morning.

Ned opened the door, and McGinty hurried inside. Ned closed the door and faced the IRA logistics head.

"Ned, I can't tell you exactly what's happening, but we're about to have another meeting. This is a bit unusual because I thought the next move was to transfer you to the horse farm.

Shamus O'Shaughnessy has come all the way from Belfast. Neal Creedon called me this morning and said they would be picking us up within the hour. There must be some new development because this is really out of the ordinary," McGinty said.

"I'm new at this high level business. I have to take your word on it. Do you have any idea what might be happening?"

"The only thing I can figure is the queen's schedule has changed. I've seen nothing in the news about her visit, or anything else that may indicate a need to alter our plans. We'll have to wait for it to sort itself out. I do know that Shamus is not reckless. He's a methodical planner and not about to do anything foolish."

"Will I be coming back here? I want to know if I should take the clothes you placed here for me."

"Good question, but I can't answer it. I tend to think we'll be back tonight. Just leave everything put."

McGinty then walked to the window and watched the street below. He knew Neal Creedon to be punctual.

Ned emptied the coffee cup and rinsed it out along with a cereal bowl and some silverware. He then went to the bathroom and brushed his teeth. As he wiped his mouth, McGinty called from the window.

"Let's go, Ned. They're here."

Without waiting for Ned, McGinty bounded down the stairs. Ned walked out behind him, closed the door and locked it. He walked down the stairs not knowing what to expect.

When Ned reached the door to the street, McGinty had already climbed into the waiting VW van. Ned walked to it and entered the side door. Instead of sitting next to McGinty, he settled into the third seat.

Creedon, seated behind the wheel, took off as soon as Ned was inside. No one said anything or exchanged pleasantries. The two men in the front were stoic and they looked straight ahead.

The van headed west, and soon they crossed into the Irish Republic. There was no problem at the border, except for a slight traffic jam of vehicles both entering and exiting Northern Ireland.

Once across the border, Shamus O'Shaughnessy turned to the two men in the rear and said, "We're going back to the monastery. There may be a need to modify our plan to kill the queen. I'm told something has come up which we'll have to consider. Everything may go as planned...then again it might not. We'll return to Derry tomorrow night.

We've alerted Thomas Larkin, and he's expecting us."

No one said anything after O'Shaughnessy spoke. They only wondered. It had to be something serious, because the execution of the plan was moving along nicely until now.

"I'm glad I mentioned to me wife that I may not be home tonight," said McGinty. His comments garnered silence.

The van headed along the same route Ned and McGinty had taken from the island.

The men could not fully appreciate the bright sunlight available for them. They'd had overcast skies for days, and the sunshine should have lifted their spirits, but it didn't.

They traveled the less than 100 kilometers without incident and arrived at Dungloe at 10:00 A.M. Neal Creedon parked the vehicle at the edge of town and the four men walked to the beach. Larkin had arranged for the same boat and coxswain who had ferried them to and from the island days before. They exchanged brisk greetings, climbed into the boat and pushed off for Arranmore Island.

The choppy seas made McGinty ill. The rolling and pitching of the small craft sent a wave of nausea over him. He felt embarrassed by his inability to meld with the seas. Soon the effects of *mal-de-mer* had him in its grips. He leaned over the gunwale and violently vomited. At the same time, he uncontrollably defecated in his trousers. The others looked away in an attempt to spare McGinty any further humiliation. As the boat pulled alongside the island dock, the pathetic figure of McGinty alarmed Thomas Larkin.

When they secured the boat, the landing party had difficulty lifting him out, but once on the dock, McGinty's malaise quickly left him. He rose to his feet and with a comical and stilted gate, followed Larkin to the bath house.

Ever the efficient and gracious host, Thomas Larkin advised everyone that he had a stew prepared. He suggested they go to the rooms they had in their earlier visit and clean up. Everyone would then assemble in the refectory in half an hour.

Ned walked the beach instead. He'd found solace there and felt a need for it again. The past few days proved unnerving. He didn't know if it was the upcoming mission or the dependency on others that had him on edge. Maybe it was the caution Larkin gave him about trust.

He had begun to shake his uneasiness when he looked at his watch. It was 1:30 P.M. and time to head back to the refectory. He turned and retraced his route to the ancient edifice which he'd come to love.

When Ned reached the dining hall, all had assembled. Two additional members were there also: Timothy Higgins and Liam Griffith. Higgins made introductions and without further word, sat down and commenced to eat. He had an unusually serious look on his face, and acted annoyed and disappointed. Ned figured serious trouble awaited them.

They ate in silence. Thomas Larkin made several trips back to the kitchen to replenish the soda bread and coffee. Sean McGinty wore fresh clothes, but didn't have much of an appetite.

When Higgins saw that all had pretty well finished, he began to speak.

"We've had some unusual developments within the last several days which might threaten our upcoming operation.

"I've called this meeting to determine if we can go forward or not. It depends on what I can learn from you today."

Everyone looked around, hoping someone had the answer, because they were at a loss as to what Higgins was talking about.

He continued.

"I asked Liam Griffith to accompany me to this meeting. Liam works in the political wing of the IRA—its covert operations. None of you have ever met him because he resides and works in England."

Everyone looked at Liam. He said nothing, but his cold blue eyes and dominating beard generated the same reaction: Liam Griffith was not a man to cross.

"Liam contracted me two days ago and passed on some disturbing information. In a way, tis a break for the IRA. On the other had, we may have sustained a terrible setback.

"Liam, I'd like you to take over," said Higgins.

Tension gripped the gathering like a vice. Larkin put his face in his hands, as though he knew what was about to happen. O'Shaughnessy sat bug-eyed, perplexed that he didn't know of any problems. O'Shea was too far down the ladder to feel any particular sentiment. McGinty sat across from Ned and next to Larkin. He shuffled about in his seat. His eyes darted back and forth like the last time they had met in the refectory.

"Gentlemen, I will be brief. There is no need for you to know any particulars of my activities.

"Recently, we have gained very valuable intelligence information from a highly reliable source in the English government.

"That information suggests that we have a traitor among you.

"What we need to know is whether he has compromised our current plans.

"Can you tell us, Mr. McGinty?" asked Griffith.

Shock rocked the hall. The men sat in stunned silence and waited for McGinty to respond. Finally he did. His voice was high pitched and excited.

"I don't know what you're talking about. You have the wrong man. You're bloody crazy."

"We have well documented proof that you are the British government's mole, Mr. McGinty. The instrument has the highest classification, but we have seen it. You have literally sold us out because they paid you, and handsomely at that!" said Griffith.

Higgins chimed in, "What we need to know, McGinty, did you tip off the Brits about our plan to kill the queen?"

Ned became enraged! He wanted to pummel McGinty because there was nothing as low as a traitor.

McGinty's eyes darted about and caught the same disdain in everyone's face.

He reacted with great speed. Without rising, he grabbed a large bread knife on the table, simultaneously pulling Thomas Larkin's neck next to the blade.

"If anyone moves, I will drive this knife into Larkin's throat.

"I'm the one in charge now. You'll do as I say."

Unfortunately, no one was close enough to the two men to act before McGinty would kill Larkin.

"You stupid blokes don't know when the game is over. You keep this war stuff going even though you've lost.

"Yes, I am the mole, and I gave up on the whole lot of you long ago."

As McGinty berated his tormentors, Ned slipped the .32 caliber Derringer from his right trouser pocket. He eased back the hammer and pushed off the safety.

He knew that if he raised the pistol Larkin would die. Instead, he pointed it under the table at McGinty hoping to incapacitate him.

In a moment of silence, Ned applied pressure on the trigger. The hammer fell, and a loud explosion echoed off the stone walls.

The bullet hit McGinty directly on his left knee. The hollow point bullet expanded and shattered his kneecap and exited his upper left thigh.

McGinty screamed in agony. The knife fell from his hand. He let go of Larkin and grabbed his knee. Before he could gather his bearings, the others were on him. They beat him savagely.

The traitor had fallen on his right side and had assumed a fetal position, grasping his mangled knee. Blood ran from every orifice on his head. He quivered and took on the pallor of near death. Broken teeth lay beside his mouth. His voice sounded garbled because they had fractured his esophagus.

Kneeling over him, Higgins screamed at the fallen man, "Did you tell them? Did you give them our plan?"

McGinty, with eyes opaque, slightly turned toward his inquisitor.

"Tell me!" screamed Higgins.

McGinty said nothing. Higgins, in a matter of fact manner, stood up, lifted his right leg and smashed his heel down on McGinty's mutilated knee.

McGinty let forth a demonic and prolonged moan. Higgins knelt down again and repeated his demand. Sean McGinty nodded his head.

"I...I told them...the...queen. You were going to kill her."

"What else?"

"I...tttold...them about Ned. Gave them...his picture. Said he'd ambush her at the farm. That Ned...killed the three soldiers...at Clady."

Higgins stood up.

"It's over boys. McGinty has done us in...set us back months, maybe years.

"Ned, I hate to say it lad, but you're a marked man. We've got to get you out of the country. They'll soon have posters in all of Ireland, north and south.

"McGinty has dealt us an incredibly damaging blow... tis true. We'll all have to go undercover. But right now, we've got to save Ned."

Higgins sat down, ignoring the prostrate and moaning figure before him. The others stood in silence. Finally, Thomas Larkin walked over to Ned.

"Thanks, Ned O'Shea. You saved me.

"I ask a favor of you, lad. Please give me the pistol."

Ned handed Larkin the small firearm and watched his expressionless face turn toward the fallen McGinty. Larkin walked to him, leaned over and placed the muzzle on the side of the prostrate man's head. He cocked the hammer and squeezed the trigger. The room reverberated with the explosion.

Silence reigned again. The men stood looking down at the dead traitor, but said nothing. There was nothing to talk about.

One by one they drifted back to the refectory table and sat down. The men just stared. While they sat there, Thomas Larkin went into the kitchen and returned with a tray laden with bottles of Guinness stout. The men smiled weakly and reached for the fortification. They hadn't had anything to ease their pain.

Higgins spoke again.

"Gentlemen, the boat will return late this afternoon. I want all, except for Ned and Thomas, to leave.

"Thomas, you and Ned bury the body tonight, here on the island.

"Tomorrow, Ned, I want you to catch the boat at nine in the morning, take a rental car we'll leave near the dock. The coxswain will have the key.

"Before we came here, we looked into passage to the States, in case something like this might happen. In two days, a Polish, freighter, the Prasden, will leave Cork for the United States. We've booked passage for you, Ned.

"Here is the envelope with the ticket and money. You will also find the name of a contact in Boston. Tis where the ship will eventually dock after a stop in St. John's,

Newfoundland. You'll be on your own from that point. Sorry, lad. When things settle down, we'll call for you."

Ned didn't feel abandoned, but rather harbored a sense of loneliness. So much had happened in so short a time. The tension hadn't let up. And now he saw it would continue.

The boat arrived near 6:00 P.M. and the four sullen men boarded it.

Neither Thomas nor Ned went to the dock; they had bid their discontented farewells in front of the monastery.

They watched as the IRA leaders walked to the dock, boarded the craft and slowly disappeared to the southeast.

"Ned, let us locate a grave site and begin to dig while tis still light. We'll bury McGinty tonight. I doubt if anyone would see us now; however, I don't want to chance a fisherman happening upon us when we have the body outside.

"You may have noticed the monks' graveyard right to the south of the monastery. Why don't we dig there" I think after the burial, we can make it look like the others," said Larkin.

"You're the best judge of that, Thomas. What you suggest sounds fine."

The two men walked to the west side of the monastery where Thomas had some tools stored in a small shed. He retrieved a pick and shovel, gave the pick to Ned, and started for the graveyard.

A series of medieval markers dotted the rise on which the monks had located the final resting place for their brothers. Some stones were broken. Most were illegible. The centuries of wind and weather had obliterated the carvings, but Ned was able to decipher some of the Latin inscriptions. They dated from the 8th century, the Gaelic-Christian golden age which gave the world the Book of Kells, the Ardagh Chalice and the Book of Durrow.

"Thomas, this is a special place. Tis hallowed ground, and I don't think we want to put the likes of Sean McGinty here. The men buried here gave much to Ireland. McGinty is something else."

"Never thought of that, Ned. I believe you are correct. Let's continue on south another 100 meters or so and find some secluded spot."

They picked up their tools and did as Thomas suggested. When they reached a saddle between two small hills, they started to dig. The area was not as rocky as the monks' cemetery, and soon they were making good headway. Ned did most of the work while Thomas kept the earth from falling back into the hole.

"I think tis deep enough, Ned. You're about four feet down. Let's leave the shovel here and return to the refectory."

Ned climbed out of the grave, dusted himself off and headed back to the monastery with Larkin.

Take some time and clean up, Ned. I will join you in the refectory in half an hour. We'll finish up the stew I made for you chaps earlier."

Again, Ned did what Thomas said. He washed and soon was back at the table which hours before had been the scene of ugly violence and deceit.

Sean McGinty's body was gone. The blood and other remnants of the struggle had disappeared too. Ned could see Larkin at the edge of the kitchen readying things for their evening meal. After a few minutes, he wheeled a small cart into the refectory. Ned looked at the steaming pot of stew and thought of a smoke stack on a tiny locomotive. And the engineer Larkin smiled broadly as he stopped next to the table.

He opened two bottles of Guinness and then filled two bowls with the hardy dish. Larkin sat down and the men ate and drank.

"Where is McGinty's body, Thomas?"

"I wrapped him in a plastic sheet and drug him back to the kitchen. After we finish eating, we'll take him to the grave. It will be the end of a rather full day, wouldn't you say, Ned?"

"Tis all very sad, Thomas...very sad."

They said little else. Both remained pensive and didn't eat with any particular verve.

Thomas lit several candles. Ned watched the shadows they'd created and wondered about the future. Where would fate take him, and when would he return? He loved Ireland. He loved the IRA and its cause. He wanted to stay with both because they gave him purpose.

"Tis time, Ned. Let us bury the dead, no matter how disgusting he might be."

They rose together and placed their dishes on the cart. Thomas pushed it back to the kitchen with Ned in trail.

When they reached the kitchen, Ned saw the body next to a door opening to the west.

Thomas opened a cabinet and took out a flashlight and then walked to the door.

"I have a wheelbarrow outside. We'll put McGinty in it and push him to his final resting place. I will lead the procession," Larkin said as a sardonic smile crossed his lips.

Together, they lifted McGinty's body and took it several meters outside. They dumped him into the pushcart and started for the grave site. Only the waves, lapping at the beach, lent any solemnity to the macabre fanfare. When they reached the grave, Ned lifted up on both handles and unceremoniously dumped the traitor into the hole. He took the shovel and filled it.

Larkin scattered similar turf and rocks over the grave and told Ned he would return tomorrow and garnish it some more.

Larkin started back to the monastery, but Ned stood for a minute and thought. He wondered how sad an ending this was for any man. There was no one to pay any last respects, no family to weep, no priest to absolve and bless. He reflected on McGinty's wife and daughters, and how they would never know what happened to their husband and father. But McGinty had betrayed the cause and got paid for it. That thought brought Ned back to reality. He understood McGinty's profane burial only proved fitting.

Soon Ned caught up with Thomas and the two walked the short distance back to the monastery.

"I've had enough excitement for the day, Ned. I'm tired, so I will go to bed. We'll have some coffee and soda bread in the morning. Good night, lad, and I thank you again for saving me life."

"You're welcome, Thomas," said Ned.

They both retired and slept well.

Ned caught the boat precisely at 9:00 A.M. the next morning. He told Thomas goodbye. They both reasoned that it might well be the last time they would see each other. Thomas was saddened about Ned and the cause. He realized too that his existence would now become uneventful, and that his life would slowly wane on the monastic island.

When Ned reached the shore, the coxswain gave him the key to the rental car. Ned climbed in and headed for the port city of Cork in the south of Ireland.

CHAPTER 7

Taking a convoluted route, Ned arrived one week later in Cork. He turned his rental car over to an IRA operative in the city and walked a mile to the wharf and looked for the Polish freighter, the Prasden. Few vessels dotted the harbor that early May evening of 1967, and he had little trouble locating the ship.

His heart sank when he saw her. Just 300 feet long, she hardly seemed seaworthy. Her rusted hulk gave off a sinister air of unkemptness and the foreboding sense of trouble.

Ned didn't want to jump to conclusions and tried to fortify his feelings with the realization that whatever the duration, the voyage would be comparatively short. All he really knew from the travel packet he'd received was that she would sail the following Friday, give or take a few days. Such ships' schedules responded to the loading of cargoes. Once accomplished, they put to sea immediately. Unlike commercial liners, passengers had to exercise greater flexibility if they booked passage on such modes of transportation, checking frequently with the harbor master on sailing dates.

Ned hoisted his duffle bag on his right shoulder and moved up the gangplank. At the top, a seedy looking merchant sailor reflecting the outward appearance of the ship stopped him. "Where you to?" he demanded in a slurred Newfoundlander accent. Taken by surprise by the other than Polish inflection, Ned immediately caught a strong odor of alcohol from the crusted lips of the deck hand. His eyes appeared glassy and his yellow, rotting teeth intermittently peeked from inside his swollen and parched mouth. Weeks at sea, a poor diet and a lack of dental hygiene told of a hard life. And when in port, he compounded his degenerate lifestyle with excess drink.

The Newfoundlander's ruddy and puffy face reflected hypertension or possibly diabetes. Whatever, Ned felt he probably wouldn't live long unless things changed, but then people don't change.

"If you're in charge, I'd like you to direct me to my cabin. I have passage to the States and would like to settle in at the earliest," said Ned.

"Cabin?" howled the drunk. "We don't have cabins on this scow. We hands bunk together two decks down, eight to a compartment!" At that point, he leaned over the railing and threw up, and then slowly slid onto the deck with the residue from his vomit running down his chin.

Fortunately, the ship's bursar, returning from liberty came up the gangway and took Ned in tow. Fastidious and effeminate in his manner, he delicately stepped over the partially prostrate seaman, making no mention of his inebriated condition, and walked to the forward superstructure. They entered a back hatch and climbed a ladder to a deck above. At the top they entered his office. Cramped, but neatly arranged, he sat at his desk and took Ned's boarding pass and checked his name off a rather short manifest.

"I am Officer Karl Herning. You, Mister Kinney (the fictitious name on his passport), and three other men have booked passage. They have not boarded yet. I hope they do so soon because we'll be underway by noon tomorrow. In the meantime, you can stow your gear in the aft superstructure. You will billet in compartment 1B. It houses four bunks." Ned immediately felt relieved that he wouldn't have to tolerate the deckhand. "You will take your meals in the officers' mess. Here is a schedule of the location, settings and the ship's daily routine. Thank you, that is all."

Ned went below to the main deck and then aft to his compartment. He found it without difficulty and placed his belongings on the lower, port side berth. A smudged and somewhat opaque porthole graced the aft end of the quarters. He walked to it and peered out. It looked directly over the fantail. "Nice view," he thought. He didn't figure he would spend much time watching the voyage through a rear view mirror, so to speak.

Hunger started to gnaw at him. Ned realized he hadn't eaten in 12 hours, yet he didn't want to go ashore. The lower profile he maintained, the better. He wondered if the Irish authorities had mustered any kind of serious effort to find him. He figured they might be watching the airports, but hoped they would bypass the likes of the Prasden.

He reached into his coat pocket and took out a small packet of candy. It would have to see him through the night. He slowly ate it and then found a nearby scuttlebutt close to his cabin and washed it down with the stale tasting water seemingly laced with some petroleum product.

He returned to his compartment and unpacked his sea bag, placing its limited contents in the drawers beneath his bunk. He reclined on the bunk and switched on the crude light above his head and commenced to read the only book he'd brought with him: *The Brothers Karamazov.*

Ned liked Russian literature, particularly the authors Tolstoy and Dostoyevsky. The conflict of good and evil in their tomes somehow related to the *Troubles* in Ireland. Life had a way of engaging man in these discords, although it seemed anymore that an amoral attitude had tended to displace it. He thought of McGinty and how he'd greedily sold out the IRA. He wondered too if the man had a conscience. Did he give any thought to those he'd betrayed, and did he reflect on the propriety of his deeds? He wouldn't ever know, so he kicked off his shoes and relaxed with book in hand. Ned read but a page when he suddenly felt overwhelmed by fatigue. The days on the run had caught up with him as he drifted into a deep and uninterrupted sleep.

He awoke suddenly to the reciprocating rhythm of the ship's engine. He sat up and felt a sudden vibration. They were underway.

Ned looked at the time. It read 7:30 AM. He went out on deck and watched as the small ship, with its one screw, slowly moved away from the docks and drifted to the middle of the channel. Increasing the rpm of the shaft, the Prasden made for the open ocean and when clear of the harbor, set a westerly course for North America.

Ned walked to the fantail and stood for a long time as he watched his troubled country fade from sight. A plethora of thoughts flooded his mind. What awaited him in America? Would he ever see Ireland again?

What would happen with the IRA? Would Ireland ever resolve its conflict and be united? He had no answers.

He returned to his cabin and sat on his bunk. At that point he noticed a suitcase on the lower starboard bunk. Another passenger must have boarded after he did, but moved in either a cat-like manner, or Ned was so exhausted that he simply didn't hear him. He wondered who he might be and if by chance he might be as obnoxious as the Newfoundlander.

Ned looked at the plan of the day which the bursar had given him the previous evening and noted the seating for the mid-day meal would commence right at noon. He had missed the breakfast setting; so again, he would have to endure the hunger which gripped his innards.

The rest of the morning he stood at various points on the main deck and rolled with the ground swells which gave the sensation that the ship resembled a cork in a washing machine. At one point he noticed the Newfoundlander he'd seen the night before busily engaged in arranging hawsers and other nautical implements on the deck and placing some of them in varied storage compartments. He looked green, and Ned wondered if the rolling seas and his hangover might be fomenting another gastric display. He decided not to find out and moved to another part of the ship.

At noon he went to the forward superstructure and up two decks to the officers' wardroom. Like most everything else on the ship, its confined conditions reminded him of a submarine. The bursar pointed to the far end of the table and motioned for Ned to sit there. Next to him sat another in civilian clothes, the man in his cabin. Before saying anything, the other officers began to drift in, one by one. There were five. They all remained standing until the captain arrived and took his seat. In halting English, he introduced each of his officers and then himself as Karl Suhaki. He then asked the names of the two passengers. Ned said he was Kevin Kinney. The other man assertively voiced, "Eamon Finnegan."

The mess steward had placed bowls of vegetables and a platter of unknown fish on the table. The captain helped himself and passed the food around. As they all started to eat, the officers began to talk among themselves in Polish. As if on cue, Finnegan began to engage Ned in English. His outgoing manner made Ned feel uneasy. He had become so suspicious of strangers, especially after the McGinty episode that he shared little information about himself. Finnegan was just the opposite. Between bites of food, he seemingly had a comment about everything. Quickly Ned saw him as a bore and readily tired of his non-stop verbiage. He said little except to ask for more bread. Famished, he felt a bit conspicuous about the amount of food he consumed. Promptly at half past the hour, the captain placed his napkin on the table and left. The other officers followed, leaving the two Irishmen alone.

Ned excused himself and descended onto the main deck, moved to the starboard side of the ship and watched the sea. Truculent and seemingly never at peace, the North Atlantic remained true to its reputation.

Ned had spent hours in solitude on the northwest cliffs of Ireland looking seaward, watching the angry waves crashing onto his land. He liked to be alone. He felt comfort in himself, sure of his convictions and beholden to no one, only the cause.

He liked biographies too, especially those of warriors. Military history enlivened his studies and remained an on-going interest to him. He sought to see if he could identify his persona with various leaders. He wondered what made them tick and what characteristics enabled them to become who they were. Ulysses Grant, the American Civil War general for example, had few friends. Maybe that's why he could make pragmatic decisions which cost the lives of many men and yet in the end achieve victory.

Field Marshal Von Mansteim was another. Always thinking beyond the immediate battles, he remained a step ahead of the Russians until Hitler's myopia overrode his field marshal's genius, and he relieved him. Lincoln trusted Grant and let him win the war. Hitler trusted few subordinates and micromanaged the war to a disaster.

Ned remained deep in thought for hours. He reflected on the command structure of the IRA and its viability. McGinty had compromised it. Were there other moles? His war didn't replicate Grant's or Von Mansteim's. Rather, it resembled the thinking of Ho Chi Mien and his efforts to unify Vietnam. What would be the IRA's path to victory? Would it remain guerrilla in nature or find a solution at some political roundtable?

Suddenly he felt a hand on his shoulder. "Shall we have some supper?" said Finnegan. Ned instinctively looked at his watch. It read 5:20 P.M. The seating began in 10 minutes. "I guess we'd best take our places at table," said Ned.

They both went up the ladder to the officers' mess and waited for the captain and the other officers to arrive. Promptly at 5:30 P.M. the meal began. It was to be a repeat performance. The officers spoke Polish and Ned said little as Finnegan said too much.

Ample portions of steaming sausage and sauerkraut filled their plates. Ned had no trouble consuming it all. Feeling satiated, he excused himself immediately after the captain left.

Instead of descending the ladder to the main deck, he went one deck up and walked to the flying bridge on the port side. He did not enter the wheelhouse, but leaned forward and watched the seas rolling in front of the ship. He experienced greater swaying motion at this height, and gently moved side to side as the small freighter rocked in the unsteady seas.

Ned remained on deck until three bells (9:30 P.M.) when he returned to his cabin. Finnegan, already in bed, greeted his cabin mate with a less outgoing manner than he'd displayed in the officers' mess.

"I see you're reading *The Brothers Karamazov*. I read it some years ago," said Eamon in subdued tones. "I liked the characters, although I don't remember all their names."

"Which ones did you like in particular?" asked Ned.

"I liked two...the atheist-lawyer-son and the father. I identify with both. I purport atheism, and like the old man, I desire to have every woman.

"I studied the humanities as an undergraduate and took an advanced degree in philosophy at Oxford. I became fascinated with the existentialists, particularly Nietzsche and Camus. To me life boils down to personal freedom. The decisions one makes are his and his alone. They carry responsibilities, but I don't get hung up with the anxiety and dread associated with them. I accept the fact that one cannot maintain extended relationships with anyone," responded Finnegan.

Ned looked with suspicion at the man prostrate in his bunk.

"That all sounds pretty heavy. I can't help but wonder what you do for a living, and what takes you to North America?" asked Ned.

"I do a good bit of freelance writing, mainly for travel magazines, short story publications and literary journals. Other than that, one might say I'm a playboy. Fortunately, I inherited a goodly sum of money from my parents and grandparents. Early on, they acquired considerable stock interests in the Middle East region when the major oil companies began discovering the incredible reserves there. As a result, I have had access to the best of schooling, Trinity and Oxford, and the money to live as I'd like. And my, have I lived!" Finnegan responded.

"Pardon me, Mr. Finnegan, but if you have so much wealth, why have you booked passage on this weary ship?"

"Good question, lad. The reason isn't simple. One might say I tired of the high end of things and wanted to experience a bit of the ordinary, like climbing Mount Kilimanjaro last year. Prior to that, I traveled the outback of Australia and then went diving along its Northeast coast. Came face to face with a Great White and nearly soiled me bloody self."

One could readily tell the 42 year old Finnegan was in good physical condition. He looked like an athlete and gave no indication of the dissolute lifestyle he purported to live. His handsome, symmetrical face, surrounded by a full head of thick, black, well-trimmed hair, touched with traces of gray, complimented this suave, sophisticated man of seeming importance. Confident of his trim, good looks and the cultural refinement attained by a superb education, he could not hide the subtle condescending manner which enshrined him. Well-read in a plethora of subjects, he could engage his audience in most any topic.

"Do you have family of any kind?" asked Ned.

"If you're asking if I have a wife, the answer is no. I never married, but I know of one bastard son I fathered, and for all I know, there are more of the same out there. I made a lot of women.

"I had a sister who died of a brain tumor when she was just 15. My younger brother, Thomas, is a physician and lives in Australia. I visited him in Sidney when I traveled down under last. He's married and has five children. His wife is Australian. Like me, since completing his education, he pretty well left Ireland for good. Our parents died several years ago, and we have but a few relatives left there.

"I took British citizenship when I studied at Oxford and haven't turned back. Some might look upon me as a traitor, but culture and excitement awaited me in the more progressive English environment. I thrived there, where I didn't see myself doing the same in Ireland. I simply have no interest in Irish politics, like the bloody IRA and their hollow efforts to unify the country.

"I just attended a reunion at Trinity in Dublin and convinced myself I had made the correct decision. My former classmates didn't ask me what I did or where I lived. So parochial in their thinking, their minds never left the city limits. What a bunch of dull bastards."

"And what do you intend to do when we reach North America, Mr. Finnegan," asked Ned.

"I don't rightly know. Surprisingly, in my world travels, I have not visited the States. I've spent time in Canada's west coast and Montreal, but from there, I traveled the Orient, and India. Then I lived in Egypt for a year before settling down a bit in Europe. I liked Spain's east coast in particular, especially the Costa de Sol. I rented a beautiful home in Palma there on the Mediterranean and successfully bedded a number of luscious Swedes and other Northern European beauties who holiday there. My luxurious accommodations and cabin cruiser afforded some of these lovely ladies to opt for my more regal settings then the pensions many had to settle for.

"In the 10 years I lived there, I had three mistresses, two Swedes and one German. They all took me for what I was and wanted no long term commitment. Aside from them, I had a number of shorter trysts. Those were probably the best years of my life to date."

Eamon Finnegan rested on his bunk with his hands behind his head. His lips took on a fragile smile as he relished the thoughts of his Palma conquests. He thought too of Dostoevsky's take on love from the author's *Notes from Underground*, namely it being nothing other than a struggle. Eamon had no time for emotional struggles. He likewise dismissed Kavanaugh's **Love's Labor** when the author cited love being "hard won through arduous relationships of covenant and trust." Who had either the time or energy to expend on such encounters? Life had brought him great amounts of pleasure and little if any sorrow or meaningful responsibility. He felt neither remorse nor regret for his ways. He wanted no commitment to a person, a cause or a country.

He had his life programmed. When he could no longer enjoy the fruits of his inheritance, whether caused by sickness or old age, he would simply commit suicide. He had researched data from the Hemlock Society and felt comfortable about his future decision; although for now, he remained intent on gleaning every bit of intellectual and physical stimuli life could offer.

"Sir, one final thought: As an undergraduate, I read a treatise by a German theologian by the name of Ratzinger. In it he said, 'The root of man's wretchedness is loneliness, is the absence of love and what man needs is communion.' I suppose that can come in the form of commitment to family, friends or comrades in arms. Does he have merit? Also, do you recall the quote from **The Brothers Karamazov** wherein Dostoevsky asks 'What is hell? I maintain that it is the suffering of being unable to love.'"

Finnegan looked at Ned pensively. "As social beings, yes, we do need communion or commitment as you say, with our fellow man, but there is a limit. And I told you my thoughts on love. Who needs that kind of drag in your life?

"I took a psychological test once, and my personality came out as **now you see him, now you don't**. I interact with people only to the point that I find them of interest, or for what I can obtain from them. I feel no commitment beyond that."

He stared at Ned waiting for a response, but Ned felt fatigued and wanted to hear no more of Finnegan's ramblings. He quietly undressed, slipped into his bunk and turned out his light. Before falling asleep, he thought of how different he and Finnegan were. It boiled down to commitment. Ned felt total commitment to Ireland and the IRA... Finnegan none to anything or anyone. How little the two had in common.

After breakfast the following morning, Ned again went to the flying bridge and spent the morning there, rolling with the small vessel as it incessantly struggled with the cruel North Atlantic.

Ned thought of the many merchant ships torpedoed by German U boats during World War II, and how the merchant seamen perished in its frigid, gray waters. He continued to wonder about why the world always seemed at war and how pitiless and inhumane it had to be. Yet, he felt no sorrow or regret for the kills he'd scored for the IRA. They gave him purpose and a great inner satisfaction...something he knew Finnegan could never comprehend.

The journey continued uneventful. Ned and Finnegan took their three meals a day and talked little. The night before the ship was to berth in St. John's, Newfoundland, Ned felt compelled to ask Finnegan a personal question.

Eamon, relaxed in his bunk reading a skin magazine, gazed up as Ned entered their cabin.

"You look pensive, lad; something on your mind," observed Finnegan.

"As a matter of fact there is, sir. Some nights back, Mr. Finnegan, you discussed your background and lifestyle. I respect your person, although I might not subscribe to all your thought processes.

"Do you mind if I ask you about something you said in one of our conversations?" queried Ned.

"Go right ahead, Kevin," Eamon shot back.

"Well, sir, you somewhat flippantly mentioned you had fathered a son out of wedlock. It struck me how fanciful you came across with this fact, and I couldn't help but wonder about the details. How did you know you'd had a son? Did you ever see the lad and what about his mother?"

Eamon spontaneously sat up and stared at Ned. The look on his face took on a demonic air. He knew Ned questioned his obligations and commitment to this event in his life, and he was ready to defend what he'd done.

"I will give it to you straight on young man. While at Trinity, I romanced a young woman by the name of Kathy O'Shea. She had beautiful blue eyes, a perfect figure and radiant black hair. I suppose it's the closest I'd ever come to actually falling in love, but seduction took precedence over love. I scored and felt mighty proud of my conquest.

"She informed me a couple of months later that she had conceived and wanted to know if we would marry. I flatly broke it off and told her no way would I commit to her or the child. I suggested that she go to England and have an abortion, and that I would cover the expenses.

"Looking back, I realize the woman had a lot of inner beauty and strength. She would not consider my suggestion and carried the child to term. I refused to see her after she had told me of the child. I simply gave her money to tide her over until she could give birth. After that, I told her she and the baby were on their own.

"I suppose what you figured I did was cruel. Yes it was, but I had an agenda and no woman or child would get in my way.

"She came to me the day after I'd graduated. She had the child with her. I must admit, he was a handsome little guy, and I had pangs of belonging, but I refused to let myself be taken in by the love crap.

"I asked the boy's name and what she intended to do with him. She said she had named him Ned, and that she had made arrangements to leave him in the care of the Sisters of Mercy at their orphanage in Wexford.

"She thanked me for providing her financial support during her pregnancy, and then called me a bastard.

"That is the last I saw of her. Two years later, while at Oxford, she wrote to me. I don't know how she got my address, but she said she had never gotten over my treatment of her and would end her life.

"I threw her letter away, figuring she wanted only to make me feel guilty, entice me to renew our relationship and eventually marry her...or get at my money. A couple of weeks later, my roommate at Trinity sent me a letter. In it he included her obituary notice. It said Kathy had died of an overdose.

"That ended that. I resolved to put her and the baby behind me. Never again would I let myself become emotionally entangled like that," concluded Finnegan.

The hair rose on the back of Ned's neck. All the pieces about his past fell into place. He immediately recalled how the Mother Superior at his orphanage called him in at age 13, before he went off to the Christian Brothers boarding school. During this terse conversation, she told him the name of his mother; that she too was an orphan; that she had struggled with giving him up; that she would not divulge the name of his father, and that she eventually took her own life.

The one-on-one left the young boy with a great sense of sadness and loneliness. Tears well up in his eyes and his lips quivered as he looked at the nun in disbelief trying to comprehend his troubled and rootless origin. The nun ended the conversation by telling Ned that to the best of her knowledge, he had no relatives. His mother had remained very private, uncommunicative and seemingly depressed.

His mind shifted back to the man before him. He glared in disbelief at his father. This rotten, irresponsible English citizen across from him nauseated him. He had robbed Ned of growing up in a normal home; he'd cast him aside like a piece of trash; he'd denied him love and support and left him with an inner void...no mother and no father. Never having experienced family life, Ned wondered if he'd been different than what he had become...a revolutionary, intent on killing and having no sense of belonging to anyone.

His hatred for Eamon Finnegan consumed him; however, he held his emotions in check. He resolved at that moment that he would kill this vile man. He did not know when or where, only that he would methodically go about it and that he would kill him.

"I guess I got more than I really needed to know, Mr. Finnegan. I didn't mean to get so personal, but thank you for being forthright with me. I hope you did not take offense to my question," Ned said stoically.

"No, I did not Kevin; however, I do not mince words. I am who I am, and I make excuses to no one and am beholden to no one," Finnegan said, as a sardonic grin etched itself on his parted lips.

"Kathy O' Shea made her call. She could not live without me and felt overwhelmed with having to rear her child alone. Her reputation soiled, she probably figured no one of worth would want to marry her. With limited skills, most likely she saw herself on the dole for the rest of her life. She didn't want that and simply checked out," Finnegan said in a matter-of-fact assessment.

"Did you ever wonder about your son, or check on him at any time?" asked Ned.

"Fuck no," said Finnegan as he climbed under the covers and turned out his light.

Surprisingly, Ned had no trouble falling asleep. Firm in his resolve to kill Finnegan, he'd become just another Brit whom he'd have to eliminate.

The next day, before the Prasden entered **The Narrows** of Saint John's harbor, Ned ate breakfast with Finnegan and the ship's officers. When he'd finished, he went to the flying bridge and marveled at the sight of some incredibly large icebergs. He easily saw how the Titanic met her demise in these very same waters. The bergs dwarfed any vessel on the seas.

The Prasden took on a harbor pilot late in the morning, and he guided the ship through the narrows and eased her next to a pier. Without fanfare, the ship's hands secured the vessel, put her gangway in place and commenced to both unload and take on cargo and fuel.

At breakfast, the captain said they would remain in port for 24 hours and then set sail for Boston. He stressed the need for punctuality because they would depart no later than that time.

Friday in Saint John's, Newfoundland...what would Ned do? As he prepared to disembark, the Newfoundland deck hand came up to Finnegan and Ned as they waited to descend the gangway.

"Do you lads want some action or do you want to sightsee?

"If you want to tour, take in the Cabot Tower...big 500th anniversary of the bloke. He discovered the island.

"Now if you'd like some adult beverages, go into town and visit the Crows Nest. The place has a German periscope taken from a captured U boat mounted in the middle of the elevated pub. You can look out over Saint John's harbor and then around in the city...quite a view in the scope. The place also has great fish and chips and a good variety of Newfoundland beers. I'd recommend Blue Star or Jockey. They both have a special bite. Of course, there's the hard stuff too, like Screech, the Newfoundlanders' drink," opined the upbeat deck hand, obviously well versed in liquid refreshments and anticipating a big night on the town.

When the two men descended the gangway and stepped onto the pier, Ned turned to Finnegan and told him he wanted some time alone and that maybe they could meet that evening at the Crows Nest. Finnegan expressed reservations and begged off with a slight hint he might see Ned later.

They parted ways and Ned ambled downtown, trying to adjust his gate to the steadiness of the land. He figured anyone would experience vestibular problems after rocking back and forth on the small Polish freighter for as long as they had.

Ned strode along the pier, looked up at Cabot Tower and decided he'd walk into the city and find the Crows Nest. He wanted a change of scenery and a chance to clear his mind, and maybe talk with someone other than Finnegan.

He ascended a rather steep hill after asking directions to the pub and finally located it amongst some winding streets and closely packed structures.

He liked what he saw. It gave off a bright and warm ambiance. The round bar sat in the middle with ample seating both there and at the numerous tables. He saw the periscope and decided a bit later he would look through it; however, for now he would satisfy his thirst.

Ned went to the bar, took a seat and ordered a pint of Jockey. The barkeep told him it only came in bottles. Ned settled for that.

He took a long slow swig of the Newfoundland beer and judged it acceptable. Not heavy like Guinness, but it had a bitter, hoppiness, similar to an India Pale Ale, which he liked.

After savoring his first bottle, Ned ordered another and nursed it along with some peanuts in a bowl in front of him. As his mind drifted off, reflecting on the startling revelation he'd encountered on the ship, a couple of sharply dressed young men took seats next to him. They seemed stiff in their demeanor and spoke in bass voices. They had very close cropped haircuts and looked out of place...almost comical. Ned hadn't had a haircut in several months and looked more in line with his age group than these two blokes.

The two men drank Blue Star and asked Ned if he minded sharing the peanuts in front of him. He obliged them and added that they had American accents and wondered what brought them to Newfoundland.

The one next to Ned said the American government had posted them to the Marine Barracks at the US Naval Station in Argentia, about 90 miles southwest of Saint John's on the Avalon Peninsula.

Ned didn't know what they were talking about. He told them he just gotten off a ship from Europe and wasn't familiar neither with Newfoundland nor with anything they said.

The two laughed and apologized for being so presumptuous. They went on further to say the United States had a naval base in Newfoundland leased by Great Britain to them in 1940, during the lead up to World War II, adding that they were Marine officers and that the Marines were responsible for the base's security.

When they asked Ned about his destination, he simply told them he had a visa to the US and that he hoped to find work in Boston where his ship would put into in several days.

He asked if either of the men came from Boston. Neither did.

One said he hailed from South Carolina and the other came from Chicago.

After finishing their one Blue Star, the two men excused themselves and left the bar. Again, Ned noted their erect posture and somewhat robotic stride. He wondered how any organization could transform men to become like this. The IRA certainly lacked this regimentation. Ned thought maybe had they had more of it, they would have weeded out the likes of McGinty.

Ned ordered fish and chips and another beer, this time a Blue Star. It tasted good too.

As Ned ate his food, he slowly devised a plan to kill his father. Their cabin stood at the fantail on the main deck. Back behind it, about eight feet separated it from the rail at the stern. Unless a third party stood there, no one could actually see what might transpire in this part of the ship.

Ned conspired to somehow lure Finnegan out behind their cabin at night and kill him. He would do this with the Derringer which he had fired into McGinty's knee at the monastery. He had brought the weapon aboard with him and had reloaded the .32 caliber two barreled pistol with 60 grain jacketed hollow point bullets. Although not large compared to the rounds of many other weapons, the manufacturer had designed them for extreme thermal penetration. Ned figured their kinetic energy would incapacitate his victim immediately, especially at close range.

Having frequently stood at night on the fantail during the voyage, Ned knew the conditions complimented his intentions. The winds and the rolling seas would create enough noise to mask the pistol's report. After shooting his target, he would simply flip Finnegan over the cable barrier and into the sea. The prop wash would suck him from view and he'd be lost in the ship's wake.

Ned ordered another Blue Star and walked to a table next to a large window overlooking the harbor. He felt anxious. Too much had happened in so short a period. A generally methodical and unemotional person, Ned had taken two body blows. First, the traitor McGinty had made him question the IRA's leadership, and now he'd come face-to-face with his heretofore unknown, egocentric father. The two incidents left him confused and wondering if any honor existed in the world. He began to question whether he'd be better served starting all over again in some remote location, like Australia. He took a heavy breath, and then a robust drag from his beer.

If nothing else he liked the solace of the window seat, but that suddenly ended.

"Say, Kevin—mind if I join you for a few drinks and something better to eat than what that mess cook has served up on that scow?" asked Finnegan as he slipped up behind Ned and put a heavy hand on his shoulder.

"Sorry, Mr. Finnegan, I've just eaten and had enough beer for the day. Don't take what I say as rude, but I need to walk for a bit by myself. I have some personal things troubling me, and I need to sort them out," said Ned in a pensive voice.

Finnegan looked surprised and miffed that someone would turn down an invitation from him. Somewhat annoyed, he bid his farewell and walked straight to the bar and began engaging some of the patrons there with his importance.

Ned didn't finish his beer, but rose and silently walked out of the Crows Nest. Finnegan watched him leave and wondered about the change which seemed to have come over his cabin mate; however, he wasn't to waste time with this unknown, pedestrian shipmate that he knew little if anything about.

The Prasden sailed at mid morning the next day. A harbor pilot deftly took her through **The Narrows** and out into the Atlantic. After exiting onto his pilot boat, the ship set course for Boston.

The sky, a brilliant blue, lifted the spirits of all hands as the small but sturdy ship churned its way southwest to the United States. After the noon meal, Ned took his usual position on the flying bridge. While dining one of the ships officers suggested they enjoy the day because a nor'easter awaited them by nightfall. The weather bureau had cautioned the Maritimes of heavy winds and seas.

"Fortuitous?" thought Ned. He figured the weather would provide a perfect cover to dispose of his father, a man for whom he had ambivalent feelings. It is only natural to love your father, but how could one love a man who had rejected you out of hand?

As the ships moved beyond the Avalon Peninsula on the southeast coast of Newfoundland, they ran into a fog bank. Ned looking into the bridge, watched as a sense of tension came over the watch officer. The forewarning of the storm became evident. In what seemed but a short time, the seas began to rise and the Prasden awkwardly began to roll in the churning waves which bellowed up from all directions.

By time of the evening meal, the storm had made its presence known. The plates on the table shifted and those present had to steady their cups from spilling and their plates from sliding about.

Everyone ate rather quickly and set about to their assigned stations to ride out the storm. Ned and Eamon returned to their cabin forward of the fantail.

Darkness began to descend on the ship as the wind worked its way to gale force. Ned suggested to Finnegan that they go to the fantail and take in the storm before they would be forced to ride it out in their cabin. Finnegan agreed and slipped on a rain coat and tweed cap which he pulled tightly about his head.

The two men, trying to gain their sea legs, worked their way to the railing on the fantail. They had to shout to one another over the churning seas and howling wind.

Finnegan made some small talk about how the Mediterranean never rivaled the North Atlantic weatherwise. He then suggested that maybe they should return to their cabin.

The window of opportunity began to close. Ned softly took hold of Finnegan's arm and moved around him so that he faced the sea and Eamon stared at the back of their cabin.

"Before we return I have something I must tell you," said Ned in an assertive tone.

Miffed, Finnegan looked at him with a perplexed expression waiting for he knew not what. A man always in total control, he now felt ill-at-ease and apprehensive because of the determined look on Ned face. Between the pitching ship and violent weather, this was not the place to be.

"Can't we continue this inside?" he queried.

"It will take but a minute," said Ned.

"Mr. Finnegan, my name is not Kevin Kinney. I am traveling under false pretense. I am an IRA operative on the run. I am an orphan and my real name is Ned O'Shea. My mother was Kathy O'Shea as I was told in the orphanage and that she had committed suicide. The time line fits your story of hers and my abandonment.

"You, you dirty bastard, are my father!"

Eamon Finnegan's mouth dropped open. For the first time in his life he didn't know what to do. A rush of emotion overwhelmed him. He felt ashamed. He almost wanted to cry and ask forgiveness, but he couldn't. He remained speechless and transfixed as he leaned against the cable railing.

Finally, his mouth quivered as he emitted a soulful moan. He had no idea what to expect next as his new found son glared at him. Whatever, he had a premonition that payback awaited him.

It happened in an instant. Ned moved against him, eyeball to eyeball and cried out in a loud voice, "You bastard! You low-life bastard! You denied me a name; you denied me love and a home; you denied me my mother, you filthy bastard!"

Without waiting for a response, Ned O'Shea pulled the .32 caliber Derringer from his coat pocket and pressed it under his father's sternum and pulled the trigger.

The bullet drove up and into his heart and killed him instantly. The kinetic energy of the bullet pressed Finnegan backwards and at the same instant, Ned put one hand on his father's neck pushing back. With the other, he grabbed a leg and flipped him over the guard rail.

Eamon Finnegan disappeared in the wake of the ship. Ned watched and could see nothing other than the churning waves, knowing somewhere down there his only living parent had exited his life.

Ned too felt a wave of emotion and he did what he did when the Mother Superior of the orphanage told him of his mother. He cried, only now his tears were those of hatred and loss.

The young man did not sleep the rest of the night, but harbored thoughts of a life that could have been but wasn't, and how it had left him as a loner, without family, friend or country.

The next morning at breakfast, Ned told the captain that his bunkmate drank heavily the previous evening and went out on deck about the time Ned secured. When he awoke shortly before breakfast, he noted that Finnegan had not returned. He wondered if he might be somewhere on the ship, or worse, feared that he might have washed overboard during the night.

The captain looked at Ned with obvious concern. The seas had become heavy and the ship was taking waves all about the deck.

He rose, got on the 1MC and alerted all crew members to search the ship for the missing passenger. He then turned to the officers, gave orders to reverse course and look for Finnegan.

Ned knew there was no chance they would find the man. He figured the captain did this to cover his backside when he filed his report of a lost passenger...just going through the motions.

The signal officer then alerted Canadian Maritime officials of the approximate grid where Finnegan went over the side. The rest was now up to chance. With a major storm underway and the likelihood of recovery remote no one held much hope that a successful search would unfold.

Ned remained in his cabin as the Prasden reversed course and went through the search drill. The captain posted extra watches and they dutifully scanned the turbulent seas for any sign of the missing man. No one saw anything.

After the ship had reached the area where the captain thought they might have lost Finnegan, the Prasden reversed course, notified Canadian authorities of the unsuccessful search and that they were now setting course for their original destination, Boston.

Ned wondered what awaited him as the ship made its way to the United States. The last month had not gone well and he hoped his luck would change.

CHAPTER 8

Colonel Jason Davis looked out over the Boston Navy Yard from his office in the Marine Barracks there. Memorabilia hung on his walls. They were silent reminders of days past...days which had brought meaning and satisfaction to his life.

It was a pleasant place to end a 30 year career, but he wasn't happy. He used to have a swagger in his step and a ready smile on his thin lips. But these traits had vanished. His receding hairline, lack of muscle tone in his vein ridden face, and a general malaise about him portrayed a has-been. His former 72 inch, 220 pound frame no longer cut an inspiring figure. Too much combat and too many disappointments had created a dispirited warrior.

A rueful officer, he'd fought in three wars; however, his most recent battle experiences had left him twisted and confused. A patriot of the highest order, he found he could no longer enjoy his nation or its citizens.

The mood of the country had gone from bad to worse. The insults and rejections his men experienced by many in the Boston community and elsewhere had left them bitter. Most were combat veterans, and they couldn't mesh with people who'd turned against the war. These citizens had belittled and mocked both him and his men, and it had made them sullen and resentful.

Many of his Marines shunned the city and remained on the base when off duty. Why go where you are abused and unwanted?

Colonel Davis empathized with them, but felt somewhat helpless in boosting the slipping morale in his command. The men went through the motions, but their élan had faded.

Davis's reflective mood came to a sudden halt on hearing a firm knock at his door.

"Enter!" he barked.

The door opened and his adjutant, First Lieutenant Michael Thompson, limped toward the colonel.

The colonel winced every time Thompson approached his desk. He epitomized so many young Marine officers of that day: mid-twenties with the eyes and countenances of men three times their age. Youthful vigor drained as reflected in Thompson's loss of twenty-five pounds. A once robust Marine now savaged. His uniform blouse hung on him like an oversized coat on too small a coat hanger. His passionless face and jaundiced skin mirrored the silent trauma of sacrificed youth.

The Purple Heart above his left breast pocket gave testament to death cheated at the hands of Navy corpsmen and doctors determined to keep him alive.

Now Thompson's future rested in the hands of a medical review board. The Marine Corps assigned him to Davis pending their decision.

"The message board, colonel," the gaunt officer said in a low and tired voice.

Thompson smiled weakly and placed the metal folder on his commander's desk.

"How are you feeling today, Mike?" the colonel asked in a tone of sincerity and admiration.

"All right, colonel, but still a little rocky," Thompson said with a half grin. "I hope that will pass as I build my strength.

"New subject, sir," the lieutenant said rather somberly. "The casualty lists are high. We have two KIA (killed-in-action) and six WIA (wounded-in-action) notifications to make. One of the KIAs is an officer. I suggest Captain Taylor make the call on the next of kin. He hasn't done one yet, and he might as well get his feet wet."

Lieutenant Thompson didn't like Captain Taylor. The captain was jealous of the junior officer's combat experience, and he went out of his way to demean him. The captain had received orders to Vietnam and was terror-stricken, all the while putting on a tough-guy attitude by harassing the junior veterans.

Colonel Davis said nothing but turned and sat gazing out his window. He sensed the April chill off the harbor and watched a lonely seagull work its way north below high cirrus clouds as he considered his adjutant's proposal. He knew Captain Taylor was up-tight and had annoyed just about everyone with his boot camp, drill instructor routine. He knew too that subordinates have a way of dealing with such overbearing superiors. Tempted to defer to Lieutenant Thompson's recommendation, he decided otherwise after reading the first release.

Looking at the message board, he saw the all too familiar *Killed-In-Action* format:

IMMEDIATE
03001Z APR 69
FM   SECOND BN FIRST MAR
TO   CMC WASHINGTON DC
        BUMED WASHINGTON DC
        FOURTH MCD PHILADELPHIA PA
        MARBKS BOSTON MA
INFO CG FMFPAC
        CG FIRST MARDIV
        FIRST MAR
UNCLAS//03040//
SUBJ; DEATH

A. SECONDBN FIRST MAR 030001 APR 69

1. 1ST LT THOMAS J KAGAN 0302 USMC

2. KIA

3. MULTIPLE GUNSHOT WOUNDS

4. 0400, 690402 SAME AS LINE 5

5. 0400, 690402 35 MILES SOUTHWEST QUANG TRI, RE-PUBLIC

OF VIETNAM

6. OFFICER'S PLATOON OVERRUN BY BN SIZED FORCE IN NIGHT ATTACK. NO SURVIVORS. TOTAL MAR KIA 29. ACTION

UNDER INVESTIGATION.

7. REMAINS LOCATED AT DA NANG GRAVES REGIS-TRATION

8. LORETTA KAGAN, 5516 MASON STREET, CAM-BRIDGE, MA.

(MOTHER). LOC OF FATHER UNK.

9. CATHOLIC. LAST RITES NOT ADMINISTERED.

10. AMERICAN RED CROSS/100 PERCENT/LUMP SUM

Colonel Davis clenched his fists and gritted his teeth. Lowering his head, he softly, yet firmly said, "Mike, I want you to make the casualty call on Lieutenant Kagan's next of kin."

"Yes, sir," the wounded officer said in an emotionless manner. Once the decision was made, the issue was no longer open for discussion. He brought his heels together, executed a less than perfect about face and started for the door.

"Hold it a minute Mike," came a fatherly tone. "I want you to do this because I knew this officer. He reported to my regiment six months before I rotated back to the states. He was a real warrior, Mike. I think it only fitting that a like person honors his next of kin by handling this casualty call. I mean that as a compliment."

By this time Lieutenant Thompson had turned toward his commanding officer. "Thank you, sir. I appreciate your confidence. Regardless of the circumstances, I still don't like doing these things. I've made two KIA casualty calls since arriving here, and they don't get any easier."

"I understand, Mike," the colonel replied, "but this one needs an experienced hand. I know I can trust you."

As Thompson left the office, Davis thought of how the two young officers were alike—totally trustworthy, courageous and loyal.

His contact with Kagan hadn't been that extensive, yet he remembered him well. Unpatronizing and fearless, Kagan projected an infectious professionalism to everyone around him. He saw similar qualities in his adjutant. Both selfless and honorable men, but now one was dead and the other about to be medically discharged.

He thought of how much the Corps will have lost. And it made him sad.

His eyes shifted to the two flags in his office. One represented his country, but he felt more affinity and allegiance
to the one of scarlet and gold.

CHAPTER 9

L ieutenant Thompson left the Boston Navy yard at 11:30 A.M. Instead of heading directly to the home of Lieutenant Kagan's mother, he stopped by the Pilot House Restaurant. He liked seafood and enjoyed the ambiance of the Haymarket area of Boston. Not from Massachusetts, he tried to make the best of wherever he resided. Besides, he needed some time to study the details of the death notification and make sure he had everything in order.

The battle-hardened officer ordered a bowl of clam chowder and a glass of water, and went over the casualty package his administrative chief had prepared for him.

Anymore, food seemed to nauseate him, most often at unexpected times. Aside from his combat wounds, doctors had told him he had Plasmodium Falciparum, a form of malaria found in Indochina. It had entered the chronic stage. They also advised him his relapses would be less frequent as he developed immunity to the disease.

The night before, he'd had another malaria attack, and he still felt the after effects. The aroma of his steaming soup tightened his stomach and he momentarily gagged. Breaking out in a sweat, he settled back in his booth and let the wave of nausea pass. He was a physical wreck, and he knew it. Only a miracle could keep him on active duty, which was something he wanted very badly.

Malarial parasites were not his only unwelcome guests. He also suffered from intestinal parasites that he'd picked up when crawling in rice paddies. Steady doses of B-naphthol and carbon tetrachloride were reducing the diarrhea and the hypogastric pain he experienced most every morning, but the large number of dying worms in his system still had toxic consequences.

He played with his chowder, sipping a few spoonfuls. It was no use; he didn't feel well, and the upcoming casualty call only added to his uneasiness. "I know this is duty," he said to himself, "but God only knows how I hate it."

Leaving the restaurant, he climbed into the green Ford sedan and headed for Charles Street with its gas lanterns and wood inlaid signs. A charming region of Americana, he thought to himself as he crossed the Longfellow Bridge and drove northwest to Cambridge.

Lieutenant Thompson felt out of his element. Harvard and other erudite centers of higher learning in the greater Boston area seemed to represent those he had nothing in common with. He envisioned his Marine Corps vehicle marked with a bull's eye, as it drew truculent looks and obscene gestures from passing students. "Why?" he wondered to himself.

The young officer turned down Brattle Street but had little time to admire the elegant old homes in Cambridge. He was carefully checking street signs.

He whipped a left onto Mason Street and brought the vehicle to a stop in front of a dark two story home. It had an ominous air about it. The opaque oval window in the front door shut out any friendly view from the street. The house appeared hollow and without warmth. Thompson wondered if this was a valid hunch or if his mind was playing tricks on him. He took a deep breath and got out of the car. He dragged himself doggedly along the sidewalk and went up the front steps to the porch.

The normally aggressive Marine hesitated and then rang the door bell. He waited. He was about to push it again when he heard footsteps inside the house. The door opened and a young man, about his age, wearing jeans, sneakers, and a sweat shirt glared at him through unfriendly eyes. A seedy beard covered his pimply, pocked-marked face. He had his hair pulled back in a pony tail and he wore a small earring. A cigarette hung from his full lips and he squinted as its fumes floated into his eyes. The two men looked at each other with distrust.

"Son-of-a-bitch," Thompson muttered under his breath, "This is the Bates Motel, and this asshole must be the old lady's son."

'What do you want, soldier boy?" came the caustic query from the self-appointed gatekeeper.

"First off, I'm not a soldier. My name is Lieutenant Michael Thompson, United States Marine Corps, and I'm here to see Loretta Kagan."

"I'll see if she's in, soldier boy," the troglodyte said as he slammed the door in the lieutenant's face and left him seething on the front porch.

Thompson stood for 10 minutes waiting for someone to come back to the door. He had no option but to do so. Insults came with the territory, and he had to be proper, regardless of the circumstances.

When he thought he'd been completely ignored and was about to return to his car, the door opened. Mister hospitality told him to come into the living room.

Passing through the foyer, he saw the living room to the left and a woman sitting in the center of a long, green sofa. The walls were red, with a black six-inch curving design at the top. Three other chairs were in the room, one being a large leather recliner into which the ill-mannered man of the house immediately flopped.

"Are you Mrs. Kagan?" asked Lieutenant Thompson, still standing at the entrance to the living room.

"Yes I am," she answered.

The woman appeared mummified. Her long, gray hair hung uncombed about her face and shoulders, and she wore no makeup on her pasty skin. Her non-descript dress was disheveled and frayed. But her mouth caught the lieutenant's attention. Its oval structure reminded him of a lamprey and made her look like some grotesque bit player in a Hollywood B movie.

Mrs. Kagan had on nylons too, but they had runs in them and were baggy.

She neither invited the lieutenant to sit down nor displayed any interest in his presence. He thought by her odd and unexpressive presence that she might be mentally unbalanced. He wanted to be anywhere but where he was.

"May I sit down, Mrs. Kagan?" he said in a firm voice, sensing that his anger might still be obvious.

"Sit in that chair," came a mechanistic answer as the woman pointed to a straight back chair close to where the officer stood.

Wanting to waste no time in what appeared to be an unreal situation, Lieutenant Thompson came right to the point. "Mrs. Kagan, I'm afraid I have some bad news. Your son, Thomas, was killed in the Republic of Vietnam the day before yesterday. His platoon was overrun by enemy forces and he died in the ensuing fight. Please accept the condolences of both the United States Government and the Marine Crops in your great loss. I wish there was an easier way to break this sad news, but there isn't. Is there anything I can do for you at this time—contact a neighbor, a priest or maybe a friend?"

"Shit-man-fuck!" the young man in the recliner blurted out, throwing his arms in the air in apparent frustration. "This fucking complicates everything!"

"Shut up, son," Mrs. Kagan said in an emotionless tone. She turned to Lieutenant Thompson and advised him to disregard her son's outburst. She then turned back to her son and told him to leave the room.

He stormed out, going directly to the rear of the house and out the back door, slamming it loudly.

His mother continued. "He and Thomas were never close. They saw life in disparate contexts, and I always found myself in the middle. This current generation is so strange and difficult to understand. One can believe in a cause like Vietnam, and the other can be totally against it. Personally, I was indifferent about Thomas going to Vietnam. You should know that I am a fatalist and therefore am not surprised at your news. You may find that peculiar, lieutenant, but you see, once young men make decisions about their lives, I am no longer a player. I must live my own life."

Speechless, Lieutenant Thompson looked open-mouthed at the woman on the couch before him. He thought he'd seen everything, but this had to be the utmost in absurdity.

All he could think about was getting out of the house as quickly as possible, so he advised the stoic woman that he would return the next day and go over funeral plans and other administrative details with her.

"I don't want you to come back tomorrow or anytime. We will conduct any further discussions on the telephone.

"I told you I had prepared myself for this moment, so I can give you some immediate direction," she continued.

"First, there will be no funeral in the greater Boston area. I want Thomas buried at the Punch Bowl National Military Cemetery in Hawaii. I had a brother killed in World War II, and he is buried there. Neither my son nor I will attend the burial. I want no more reminders of this tragedy.

"Secondly, I want nothing given to the media about Thomas's death. I will deal with friends and relatives in my own way.

"And lastly, how much do I get?"

"I beg your pardon, ma'am?" Lieutenant Thompson asked in disbelief.

"There must be some kind of insurance the government pays when a soldier is killed," she tastelessly responded.

"Mrs. Kagan, there is a death gratuity of $50,000 paid to those designated by the deceased. In the case of your son Thomas, he elected to have the Red Cross receive the full amount. Why he didn't designate you as the beneficiary, I do not know. We can only act on what is contained in his official records."

The woman on the couch showed the first signs of any emotion at the lieutenant's response. Slowly, her face grew taut; her body stiffened and her lips parted in an odd manner, displaying the longest teeth Thompson had ever seen in a human face. She glared at him and appeared as though she might lunge off the sofa and assault him.

Clenching her fists, she made a guttural grunt that sounded like it came from some possessed creature.

Finally she spoke, her phlegm-filled words appalling the already startled Marine. "Get out of my house you sorry bastard! Leave now!"

Lieutenant Thompson quickly rose from his chair and, without looking back, walked directly to the front door and left the house. He struggled down the front steps and reached his car. He leaned against it and threw up.

CHAPTER 10

The next morning, Lieutenant Thompson worked the message board. He made clarifying notations on subjects the colonel would question and culled irrelevant dispatches.

At 8:00 A.M. he knocked on the commanding officer's door and heard the familiar voice directing him to enter.

"Good morning, sir. I have the latest messages. There's nothing out of the ordinary, like the recent casualty cases—mainly routine stuff."

Looking up from his desk, the colonel's eyes widened when he saw his adjutant.

"I don't mean to sound like a broken record Mike, but do you feel all right?" he asked.

"No sir...I'm hung over, badly. I overdid it last night, and it was more than my system could take. I was up most of the night. That and another malaria attack left me weaker than usual."

"It's a bit out of character for you, Mike; I mean the hangover. Is there something wrong?"

The lieutenant felt a wave of uncertainty. Yes, he was troubled—very troubled, but the Corps had trained him to work out his own problems and only confide in superiors as a last resort. Besides, he was a private person and he didn't find it easy to talk about personal feelings.

"Sort of sir," came his reply. "I'd had kind of a rough time yesterday, and by last evening I was pretty confused. When I was in 'Nam, it was all cut and dried. Everyone knew his job. There was no dissension, and all hands pulled together.

"Back here I feel like a bastard at a family reunion, and I don't seem to care much about anything anymore. And the loneliness, it's as if I'm on a different planet. I can't seem to relate. This all came home when I made that casualty call on Lieutenant Kagan yesterday. It was the straw that broke the camel's back. After that fiasco, I don't remember much."

Lieutenant Thompson felt embarrassed. He had no intention of speaking to the colonel the way he had. He knew his boss had more on his mind than the grievances of some junior officer. But he was wrong.

"Sit down Mike," the colonel said as he motioned for the officer to take a seat on the couch to the left of his desk. "What was it about the Kagan case that upset you?"

"I just wasn't ready for what happened, sir," Lieutenant Thompson said, looking down at the floor.

"What do you mean, Mike?" the colonel probed.

"Sir, I know the country has become indifferent toward the war effort. In fact, I see more outward hostility against it than ever before. But it seemed to reach a new high yesterday afternoon—I mean the indifference. I just wasn't ready for what I experienced. Anyway, I ended up stopping at a small tavern close to my apartment and tried to figure out what was going on with me. The rest is history, but I did make it in this morning," Mike said with a wilted smile passing on his pale lips.

"I knew Lieutenant Kagan, Mike, as I indicated to you yesterday. Therefore, I'm really concerned about what was strange about the call on his mother. Did she come apart... go ballistic? What happened?"

"Sir, it isn't how you might imagine—just the opposite. I think Mrs. Kagan is some kind of a nut.

"I've made these casualty calls before. Each time the next-of-kin reacted as you'd expect: intense grief, sometimes with hostility, or even love. I became very close with one family while processing their son's case. But Mrs. Kagan didn't react in a predictable way. In fact, she didn't react at all— she just gave me the heave-ho.

"What upset me the most was her total lack of emotion. I wondered at the time if she and I were on the same page. When I told her Thomas had died in battle, she looked at me as though I'd advised her what time of day it was. Something isn't right about this one.

"She had another son with her, sort of a derelict looking toad who let out anger but no sorrow.

"It was really odd, colonel. She made some goofy comment about being a fatalist and being resigned to her son's death.

"She wants him interred at the Punch Bowl in Hawaii. Apparently she has a brother buried there.

"She's not going to the funeral either.

"Colonel, this family showed no love for Thomas Kagan. They were as dysfunctional as one could ever imagine. I wondered if I was in the right house, and whether she was really his mother.

"Pardon me, sir, but all the bitch really seemed concerned about was how much insurance money she would get. When I told her Thomas had not elected to give her any, she blew her stack and threw me out of the house.

"That's when I went to the bar. I've never seen anything that cruel. All I could think about was that Marine who'd given his life, and nobody cared, most of all his family. I just couldn't accept it. I still can't," Thompson concluded.

The two officers sat in silence for what seemed a long time—each sensing the other's discomfort. Finally, Michael Thompson's eyes welled up with anger and frustration. When that happened, he slowly lowered his head and silently wept. Only a slight heaving of his shoulders gave away the inner conflict which tortured him.

"Let it out, Michael. It's all right," the colonel said.

Lieutenant Thompson felt like a wimp, but he couldn't help it. Then he heard the colonel speak, his voice firm yet benign.

"Michael, when I fought in the Pacific in World War II, my mother sent me newspaper clippings and letters about the war effort back home. Everyone participated because the whole nation wanted to win.

"She told me about the victory garden they had in the backyard, and how they crushed tin cans and turned them in for war production. How all the children bought 25-cent war stamps and put them in books. When they filled a book, they turned it in for a $25 war bond.

"My dad was an Air Raid Warden. He proudly wore his World War I style helmet, painted white, around the block during drills and ensured everyone was off the streets. The ludicrous part about it was that we lived in Nebraska, and the Germans and Japanese hardly had the capacity to lob a bomb or do anything else that far inland. Regardless, they all played the game.

"I received a letter from my little brother after I'd been hit on Iwo Jima. He said the family had taken a drive by Fort Crook, Nebraska, and he waved to some German prisoners being held there. He said they waved back and smiled and mentioned how strange that all seemed to him. I guess he couldn't believe the enemy was human too.

"When I came home, the appreciation of the nation showed everywhere. I couldn't have been more proud to be an American, because the war had affected everyone.

"Not so today, Michael. I think Korea set the stage for Vietnam as far as public attitude is concerned. They call it—Korea—the forgotten war, and that's because it didn't impact the whole nation. Too many Americans continued their daily lives uninterrupted. They didn't have to make any sacrifices. At least that's my opinion. After Korea, we casually watched as the French lost at Dien Bien Phu in 1954 and the war in Indochina turned into a monstrosity. In a sense, Michael, the French provided a preview of coming attractions. Their citizenry became indifferent to the conflict. After all, most of those fighting were Foreign Legionnaires, made up of former German soldiers from World War II and other nationalities. The French nation's indifference cost them the war and a lot of men's lives.

"Had we lent them a hand in 1954, we might have prevented what's happening now.

"Michael, we have a kinship with the Legionnaires of 1954. Our nation doesn't care either. Many of our citizens have turned indifferent or worse yet, against us.

"One would like to strike back, but he can't. He can only endure because he has taken an oath to his country which he cannot violate.

"The brother of Thomas Kagan has taken no oath. He feels superior to all of us. He's a spoiled child who has all the answers; to him and the others like him, Michael, we have become the fools in a sense.

"We are burying Marines everyday because they've obeyed the laws of the country. They didn't want to die, but they knew their nation required subservience to a higher authority.

"The draft-dodgers and professors who pontificate the reasons for not serving really deceive no one. Come to think of it, I bet every time one of the chicken-shit bastards takes a shower he has to feel twice to see if he has any balls."

A faint smile crossed Michael's face. Colonel Davis was earthy, yet compassionate and well-read. He didn't like the way society had turned anymore than Michael did, and he too felt powerless to affect the outcome. But he could only persist and remain obedient to the laws of the nation, regardless of the direction they might jerk him. He felt he belonged to the only disciplined element left in American society.

Lieutenant Thompson knew the window Colonel Davis had given him had closed, so he thanked him for his time and started to leave.

"Take the rest of the day off, Michael. You look like death warmed over, and I don't want to bury any more Marines than I have to this month. Go to bed and take care of that body."

"Thank you, sir. I appreciate your counsel. It helped more than you might think."

The lieutenant left, and after giving some administrative direction in the outer office, departed the barracks, drove to his apartment and went to bed.

CHAPTER 11

The graves registration unit at Da Nang, South Vietnam shipped Lieutenant Kagan's remains to Hawaii three days after his death. Navy mortuary facilities on Oahu held the body, as directed by Headquarters Marine Corps, and made arrangements for his burial in the National Military Cemetery there.

Michael Thompson forced himself to dial Loretta Kagan's number, and on the third ring she answered.

"Mrs. Kagan, this is Lieutenant Thompson. I'm calling to advise you of the status of your son's burial."

There was silence on the other end. Finally came a, "Well?"

"Ma'am, authorities will bury Thomas at the National Military Cemetery on Oahu tomorrow.

"I will send you a copy of the message detailing the burial site, grave number and the chaplain's name, should you like to correspond with him."

Again, there was a momentary pause...then, "I don't want to communicate with any chaplain!"

Silence.

"Do you have any questions Mrs. Kagan?"

"No—why should I?"

"I thought you might want to arrange for some flowers or have some Masses said, or something to honor your son's death."

"Listen moron, if I need any guidance from you on how to handle Thomas's death, I'll ask for it. In the meantime, how about keeping your mouth shut.

"You, by the way, are getting to be a real pain in the ass!"

The phone went dead and the adjutant felt offended.

Shortly thereafter, on April 7, 1969, a detachment from the Marine Barracks, Pearl Harbor buried First Lieutenant Thomas Kagan with full military honors on a beautiful and bright spring morning atop the high ground overlooking Honolulu and the Pacific Ocean. It seemed too nice a day for a funeral; however, the ephemeral notes of the bugler's taps, softly floating over the cemetery, changed the setting to one of hushed sadness.

"The Honolulu Advertiser" carried stories about Vietnam, tourism, and the island's weather. It made no mention of Thomas Kagan's burial in the Punch Bowl.

As the burial detail lowered the casket, a Catholic chaplain blessed it and recited the prayers for the dead. No one, other than the Marines and he, witnessed this final act in a man's existence, except for a few passing tourists who gawked and took pictures from a distance.

At the end of May, the Railway Express Agency delivered Lieutenant Kagan's personal effects to the Marine

Barracks, Boston, Massachusetts. The supply chief signed for them and advised the adjutant they'd arrived, along with those of several other Marines killed in the same time-frame.

Lieutenant Thompson then called Loretta Kagan for what he hoped would be their last conversation.

"Mrs. Kagan, this is Lieutenant Thompson at the Marine Barracks. I wanted to advise you we have your son's personal effects here, and I'm wondering when we can deliver them to you."

"I don't want them Mister Thompson! I will have no reminders of Thomas in my house. I've put all that behind me. Furthermore, I trust you will never bother me again with any of this foolishness."

"Foolishness, Mrs. Kagan? I'm not sure I understand, but I will honor your requests, and to the best of my knowledge, this will be our last conversation."

The receiver went dead.

Lieutenant Thompson instinctively held it away from his face and looking at it said, "You bitch!"

He slammed down the phone and walked down to the bottom deck of the barracks to talk with Gunnery Sergeant Elsworth Hawkins, a grizzly and truculent looking 28-year veteran who appeared far older than his 46 years. An immoderate life style, coupled with the physical rigors of a Marine Corps career, had taken their toll. His wrinkled face and ashen colored skin disclosed a smoker's pallor—or perhaps something worse.

"Gunny, the next-of-kin doesn't want Lieutenant Kagan's personal effects, so let's bust open his footlocker and inventory the contents. We'll let the colonel decide what to do with any personal papers. The other gear you can put back into the supply system or give to the Salvation Army.

Together, the two men unsnapped the two latches on the footlocker and tried various skeleton keys on the flush lock. After several tries, the hasp popped up and they lifted the lid.

Both men stood perplexed at the meager contents. The shelf held a few postcards, apparently from an R&R trip, some military and civilian belts, a razor, and several pocket Westerns.

Removing the tray, they found two pair of civilian trousers, shoes, skivvies, two short sleeved shirts, jungle boots and a Marine utility uniform.

At the bottom of the box, they uncovered a dog-eared and mud splattered 11" x 14" legal pad, filled with writing.

"Wonder if it's a diary?" asked Gunnery Sergeant Hawkins.

"I don't know Gunny, but it looks like it's the only thing we need to show the colonel. The rest of this stuff isn't worth $50."

He took the pad in his hand and slowly climbed the stairs to his office. Once at his desk, he took out a large manila envelope and placed the legal pad into it, writing on the front of the envelope "Only thing of significance found in Lieutenant Kagan's personal effects."

Colonel Davis had meetings until early afternoon, so Lieutenant Thompson left the envelope on the commanding officer's desk.

When the colonel returned to his office, he relaxed for a moment. Staring out his window at the USS Constitution, tied to its moorings in the Navy Yard, he marveled at her size and speed. She sailed at 13 knots, faster than World War II LSTs. She continued as a source of pride for the nation, at least until the late 1960s anyway. Now he wondered if anything associated with the military could foster pride among the American people.

He had just returned from a civic meeting in downtown Boston. Before it started, a young woman had smiled at him, and then subtly flipped him the bird from across the room. He tried to ignore her, but the insult cut deeply. He realized he was becoming cynical, and he was afraid he would infect his command with the inner loathing he harbored for the nation's lack of understanding and patriotism.

He wondered too how he could ever move from the Marine Corps—his home for 30 years—into this civilian community, which neither understood the warrior nor cared about what he'd done. He thought of retiring to Central America, living in seclusion along its beaches, fishing by day and brooding over a glass of rum by night. He wanted to go anywhere but into the political turmoil which racked the nation.

Since the Tet Offensive in 1968, he'd seen the country's attitude change, and it began to show in the young Marines assigned to Vietnam. Too many of them concentrated on drugs rather than unit cohesion, and their lack of respect for authority cut away at the fabric of the Corps. He felt particularly distressed when he rotated back to the states, knowing those regulars staying behind had a terribly difficult task facing them.

He tried to shake off his somber mood as he unbuttoned his green, ribbon- bedecked blouse and hung it on the coat rack by his office door. Returning to his desk, he sat down and started through the papers on his desk. After signing a few routine pieces of correspondence, he came across the manila envelope his adjutant had left several hours before.

Instinctively, he felt afraid to open it. Did it contain privileged information that he had no right to see? This didn't belong to anybody, but rather to someone he knew. He took a shallow breath and slit open the envelope with his replica bayonet letter opener.

He removed the legal pad, stared at it for a moment, and then realized the writings contained the thoughts of a young officer subjected to heavy combat.

Without going further, he reached for the telephone and dialed his home. It was 3:30 P.M.

"Colonel Davis's residence, Molly speaking," came the formal answer on the other end.

Colonel Davis smiled and felt a sense of pride at the warm and courteous inflections in his daughter's voice. She was becoming a real lady.

"Molly, this is Dad."

"Oh, hi Dad. I just got home from school. Mom isn't here. She's at Jim's ball game. I guess you wanted to talk with her?"

"Yes I did, Molly. Tell her I won't make it for supper—something has come up. What's new at school?"

"Not a whole lot. We have a big literature test tomorrow, so I doubt if I can see Jim pitch today."

"Okay, pass the word to Mom, and I'll see all of you later."

He hung up the phone, regretting the years he'd lost in his children's lives. He'd spent so much time away from them. Yet they had developed into fine young people, thanks to their mother and their support and understanding for what he did.

He thought too of the insensitive remarks he'd heard that afternoon from some of the city's young movers and shakers. They overtly mocked the "military mind" like it belonged to some Neanderthal creature, capable of only grunts and unimaginative thoughts.

They had neither appreciation nor understanding of the time he and the other service officers at the meeting had devoted to the nation's defense, and none of them would ever consider a job with such demands. They were all assholes in his mind; however, he had no option but to ignore their vacuous inferences.

Coming back to the task at hand, Colonel Davis called the outer office on the intercom and left word he didn't want anyone disturbing him. At that, he picked up the deceased lieutenant's legal pad, tilted back in his chair and began to study the smudged and discolored text. Within moments, he mentally found himself transported into a world he knew so well. He could almost hear the report of automatic weapons and detect the sweet, sickening smell of burning human flesh—Thua Thien Province, South Vietnam. It began, "I killed a man..."

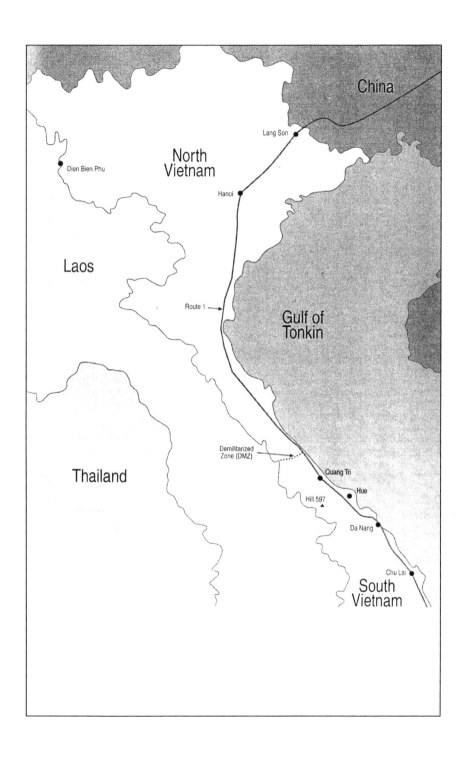

CHAPTER 12

I killed a man several hours ago. I shot him in the chest at close range with a 12 gauge shotgun. All nine pellets from the 00 buck shot shell hit him. They nearly cut him in half.

I looked at his body in the light a short time ago. He was a Viet Cong sapper. He carried a bag of explosives and a pistol, and he looked about my age. Flies were all over him.

The sun came up about an hour ago. Everything looks different now. The past six hours appear more like an aberration. I suppose because night ambushes sap your physical and emotional strength, especially when you've had a kill.

I've submitted my after action report and am exhausted, but I cannot sleep. I'm very much alone. My men have crapped-out around our company perimeter, oblivious to the rising heat and the crawling, biting insects. They only sleep, yet I cannot. My guts churn, but I feel empty inside.

Out of necessity, I write my thoughts down because it is the only way I can purge my soul. And I must if I'm to retain any sense of balance. I have fought in the bush for 15 months now. I feel the camaraderie of the other Marines, yet a separation remains. They really do not know who I am, or the thoughts that plague me. To muse over dying without purpose or direction in this wretched place, so far from my home, overwhelms me at times. It would be as though I'd fallen off the face of the earth, lost forever in history, known to no one.

I have suffered two wounds. Death seems to be stalking me. The first time I took a round along the side of my head and ended up recuperating for two weeks on a hospital ship, the USS Repose. The second time, shell fragments hit me in the shoulder, and our battalion surgeon sutured the wounds and kept me at the battalion aid station for three days. He gave instructions to my platoon corpsman to change the dressings daily and to make sure the area stayed clean. That was a month ago; they have pretty well healed now.

I signed papers before I came in country that I didn't want my "mother" back in Boston notified in case I became a casualty. I gave as a reason her poor health and my "father's" absence.

So far she doesn't know of my wounds. Every so often though, I find myself ill-at-ease about my lack of outside communication. My company commander approached me two weeks ago when we returned from a battalion-sized operation. Coming back to the rear area meant much to everyone—mail call, beer, showers, clean clothes, a flick and sleep.

Anyway, my skipper, Captain Klein, said he'd noticed I'd never received any mail. He broached it in a rare moment that found the two of us alone.

He caught me off guard, because I thought only the other lieutenants might have had a hunch, but not the skipper. He makes it a point to know his men and he looks out for our welfare. The company's morale makes the difference between success and failure, and I know he doesn't want one of his officers preoccupied with state-side problems.

Besides, our company first sergeant went off his rocker two months ago when we returned from a particularly bad operation, and he hadn't received a letter. We took 27 casualties, nine of them KIAs. Everyone was about spent, and we all looked forward to a stand-down.

When we marched to the battalion rear, they held mail call. The first sergeant hadn't heard from his wife in over a month, and there wasn't a letter waiting for him. He came apart like a dollar watch, attacking the mail orderly, claiming he hid his letters and was trying to get even with him.

After decking the guy, he tore into his mail sack, frantically searching for a letter that wasn't there. He collapsed in an emotional heap, sobbing like a baby. He didn't have a letter because his wife was screwing somebody new.

The Red Cross verified six days later that she had filed for divorce.

Our battalion surgeon gave him a shot that day and issued him a long sleeve sport coat. That's the last we saw of him. Later, we heard they had him in a rubber room at the Naval hospital on Guam recovering from an acute anxiety reaction. Where he went from there I don't know.

Captain Klein rhetorically asked if I was married: He knew the contents of my Record of Emergency Data as well as I did. I told him I wasn't. He then wanted to know if I had a girl. Again, I said no.

He continued, "You extended after your first 12 month tour. You're three months into your second tour. You didn't take any leave between tours but just stayed in the field. I've commanded this company for eight months now. I know you in a sense, but then again I don't know you at all. You're a killing machine if I've ever seen one. Sometimes you scare me by your coldness toward the daily death and destruction. You show little emotion except anger. What are your plans when you rotate back to the states?"

I said I hadn't thought that far ahead. He looked at me, half perplexed and half angered, and said he guessed I didn't want to talk about myself. I told him I didn't.

He's a good company commander, but I didn't like him getting personal. And I didn't like the shade tree evaluation of my persona. I had enough on my mind without somebody trying to play head games with me.

I think it bothers him that I don't confide in him. He's a mustang. Came up through the ranks and he has an awful lot of years in the Corps for just being a captain. He fought on Iwo Jima and in Korea. He's seen it all—been wounded, decorated, served the Corps all around the world. The guy eats, drinks and breathes the Marine Corps. I've never seen such dedication, and I respect it.

Everything he does is selfless. It's all for the Corps. There's nothing Machiavellian about him. He's simple to a fault. I suppose he's hit his terminal grade, and that won't make any difference to him. He's only in it to serve the Corps, and when he sees the likes of me, someone he can't put a finger on, it bewilders him and upsets the necessary balance he needs to command.

Captain Klein sees everything as black or white. The gray areas confuse him, and he backs away from them at every opportunity. But gray areas envelope the whole of Vietnam. Except for those of us fighting here, no one else really cares...I even wonder if the Vietnamese do?

During my first tour, we operated well south of here in Quam Nam Province. My unit, Golf Company, 2d Battalion, 1st Marine Regiment held an operation along Highway 1, or the Rue Sans Jua, "Street Without Joy" as the French called it.

I remember going into this small hamlet of only eight to 10 hutches. I entered one with my Vietnamese interpreter. An old woman squatted on an earthen deck. Aside from a rice laden clay vessel and a dwarf-sized wooden bed, she appeared to have few other possessions.

Excited and apprehensive, she kept looking at me and rapidly talking with my interpreter, waving her arms about and displaying obvious displeasure with us being there.

Finally, my interpreter turned to me and said, "She thinks you're going to take her rice." I told him to tell her to relax. We wouldn't take anything and would be in the area just a short time.

She flashed a toothless smile at his words of assurance and then began another animated discussion with him, only more upbeat. After a few minutes, Warrant Officer Nuyen turned and said, "Lieutenant, she thinks you're a French Legionnaire." My heart sank.

That night a billion stars must have graced the heavens. The lack of light heightened their brilliance—a truly magnificent sight.

After checking my platoon's positions at 0200, I sat on the deck, leaning against a wheel on a jeep trailer and looked up into the beautiful sky. I couldn't sleep, but rather wondered about the old woman and how ignorant she and the other people here must be. The French lost at Dien Bien Phu in 1954. Here it is, the late 1960s and this old lady didn't even know they'd left. I guess at that moment I knew the Americans were working on a lost cause. The people didn't care; they just didn't want us to take their rice.

This wouldn't have bothered Captain Klein. He could only see the Marine Corps mission here. Nothing else mattered. Keeping things on that plain sure reduces any self-doubts.

The captain refuses to enter any conversations when a new lieutenant reports into the company. Often they bring stories from the States about the anti-war movement, and how these college draft dodgers demonstrate against the government and try to turn it upside down. They even told of ones attending foreign universities and holding anti-war rallies there.

We all would listen in disbelief, and wonder how anyone could do that and leave his mates to fight the war.

During such discussions, the captain sloshes coffee around in his canteen cup and takes on a 1,000 meter stare. He only talks about Marine Corps related topics. He knows nothing else because he reads only military manuals; however, one would find it hard to disparage this one dimensional man.

Despite his inability to relate on an intellectual level, he understands men in combat and can identify with their plight in a compassionate and understanding way.

A tough, pedestrian man, he pulls no punches and remains up-front with everyone. He has no hidden or sophisticated agenda that might lead one to false impressions. In times of sustained combat, such a quality means much to unit cohesion. The men will follow him anywhere. They know he cares more for them than he does for himself. He's a limited officer, yet a magnificent leader.

I've had the same platoon the whole time I've been here. It's the third. We affectionately refer to ourselves as the "Third Herd."

All the men in my original platoon either rotated back to the States or were killed, or wounded and evacuated. Their replacements filter in periodically, normally about one or two a week, depending on the casualty rate, but we somehow retain our identity.

I usually take each man aside and speak at length with him about his home, aspirations, and other concerns. Hopefully, they do most of the talking. I want them to know I'm approachable and will listen to them. They appear better educated as of late, but exhibit some of the indifference and lack of belief their college contemporaries espouse. Funny though, once in the platoon, the others isolate them if they evidence any condescending attitude. It doesn't take many skirmishes before they realize that if they survive, they aren't going to do it on their own.

Staff Sergeant Chester A. LaCount, my platoon sergeant for the past 11 months, hails from Thibodaux, Louisiana and speaks Cajun French. Two other men in the platoon from Louisiana speak Cajun too.

He will rotate home next month unless he extends, which I doubt if he'll do. He is married and has two daughters, and I know he misses his family very much. He's also highly committed to the platoon, so he's confronted with a dilemma: "Do I rotate or extend?" He asked me about it before our last operation. I told him he'd done his part and to go back to his family because they needed him too. If he wants to stay, he knows I'd be more than glad to keep him aboard.

So far, Staff Sergeant LaCount hasn't been wounded. A wiry man with a high energy level and weighing about 140 pounds, he's always on the move, seeing to the needs of the men and kicking ass at the appropriate times. The men love him and seem habitually entertained by his caustic tongue, laced with Cajun jargon. He's almost like a boxer; he has all the right moves and is a step ahead of the men. But most of all, they love him because he's courageous and exhorts them to do their best and to be brave too. He, like Captain Klein, neither knows nor wants to know anything other than the Marine Corps. And how fortunate the Corps is to have such dedicated men.

I mentioned our company commander. The other officers represent a mix, but all are college graduates. Two came from the Naval Academy, one from Holy Cross, one from USC and my records show me as a Boston College graduate.

Our executive officer, Brad Lemke, is the USC grad. He's on the list for captain and will rotate back home in three days, about the time I go on R&R to Singapore.

Fred Morely commands the first platoon, went to Annapolis, and sometimes I think he wishes he'd gone Navy. Here just three months, a fog kind of surrounds him. He got married right after graduating from the Naval Academy, and in less than a year, the Corps sent him here.

He's smart, but uptight. He lost six men in the last operation, and it rattled him. He's resourceful, and I think will eventually overcome his current restraints. He broods too much about his wife.

Fred's Annapolis classmate, Arthur Cook, has the second platoon and is just the opposite. He's loose and unflappable, a great physical specimen who drives his men hard and has a good time doing it. I always like it when he's on my right or left flank because he's so level headed and dependable. Even in the worst of conditions, he always has time for a smile.

Ken O'Brien from Holy Cross has the weapons platoon. He's a good guy, sort of like a mother hen. He usually has his machine guns attached to the rifle platoons, but he is always around. He's a mechanical wizard and can fix any weapon on the spot. His guns always sound like sewing machines. They purr in alternating and rhythmical six round bursts, delivering tremendous volumes of fire right on the targets. He really has his men trained.

Ken wants to become a lawyer when he leaves the Marine Corps.

That is a cross section of our company and its leaders. We always are under strength. I'm supposed to have 44 men, but I usually have between 30 and 35. Even though we're at reduced in numbers, we fight well.

I'm looking forward to my Singapore trip. I long for the time away from my platoon and Vietnam. The months have been hard, and the batteries need charging. Five days with no responsibilities and plenty of sleep should give me a new lease on life. Right now, I just slug it out from day to day; my mind has gone into neutral and my instincts have taken over. I know my senses are keen, and at times I feel like an animal: I'm either stalking or being stalked.

CHAPTER 13

My day for R&R finally came. Catching a hop on a supply chopper at 0600, I flew to the Marble Mountain helicopter pad outside Da Nang and caught a ride to the main airstrip west of the city. There I checked into the R&R office and after processing, waited for the flight to depart.

Late in the afternoon, the Marine at the desk announced the boarding of our flight. We filed out to the plane, an old PanAm DC-6, and quickly went up the ladder and found a seat.

My only concerns were whether the plane might take a hit from enemy fire, or have mechanical problems before we got underway. But my worries were ill-founded; before long we headed south out over the South China Sea and started our trip to the island nation of Singapore.

Several older stewardesses passed out warm, moist hand towels so we could wipe our faces and seemingly remove any traces of Vietnam. Then they started to serve drinks.

The mood in the plane seemed unusually constrained. For whatever reasons, the men kept their thoughts to themselves. We made it out of Vietnam, but in five days we would return to the war. By the time everyone started to unwind and adjust to life without fear, we'd be right back into it. One doesn't turn emotions off and on like a faucet.

A fellow platoon commander, Jim Hanks, proved that during my first combat tour. He wrote me after rotating back to the States and told me of the difficulties he had adjusting to civilian life. He said he couldn't cope and kept having nightmares. His wife didn't understand him, and his daughter feared him. He felt he'd have trouble holding a job because he couldn't liken himself to the insouciant attitude of the masses. He said the country acted as if it didn't know it was at war; that folks regarded him as a freak.

A month later I received a form letter, apparently sent to everyone in his address book, stating that he had killed himself.

Our plane landed in darkness. It was 2200 Singapore time. The R&R authorities herded us off the plane and into a confined reception area to brief us on local customs, tell us where we could stay and what we could and could not do. They had an R&R hotel designated for us and the rooms were $5 a night. The officer-in-charge suggested we stay there at least the first night.

A beautiful Eurasian girl sat to one side. She was part of the Singapore Tourist Commission or something. After the R&R pukes finished apprising everybody about the cost of tail, VD rates, and where you could take a whore (the R&R hotel one of them), she proceeded to tell us all about the wonderful city and things to do. It must have embarrassed her, talking to all these hormone-laden troops who paid little attention to what she said.

Then we boarded the busses for the R&R hotel. By this time I was exhausted and wanted nothing more than to shower and climb between clean sheets and sleep for about 12 hours. But it didn't happen.

The R&R hotel resembled a fraternity house on Friday night. Drunken Marines were yelling and running up and down the passageways, chasing their hookers and blowing chow all over. The guy in the room next to mine was banging some gal one minute and then having a fight with her the next. I slept little.

The next morning I checked out as quickly as I could and hailed a taxi. Once inside the cab, I asked the driver about the best hotel in town. He liked the Singapora. I told him that sounded fine and to just get me out of here.

As we rambled along the amazingly clean streets and through orderly traffic, I marveled at the difference in prosperity between Vietnam and Singapore. When a nation can direct industrial energies toward peaceful efforts, the results are immediate and obvious. Too bad Vietnam couldn't do this.

I don't remember how long we drove. I was deep in thought when my driver stopped in front of a stately edifice and informed me we had arrived at the hotel.

I paid him, took my small bag, exited the cab, and stood momentarily in the brilliant morning sun. It had rained earlier and everything seemed fresh and clean. I had started to relax, not suspecting that when I walked into the building in front of me, my R&R would become another war zone.

I opened one of the large glass doors to the hotel's lobby. The cool interior, with its ceiling fans spinning and potted plants tastefully positioned around its marbled decks, made me think I had entered some type of resort.

I walked to the counter, and a well-dressed Chinese man in his 50s looked up from his desk with a hesitant expression. I probably appeared pretty hardened, and I could tell he was reticent to have me as a guest. They obviously catered to a classier crowd than the pedestrian type I represented. But money talks, and when I said I would pay in advance, he lessened his condescending air. I registered without further concerns.

I told the clerk I wanted a quiet room not facing the street. He gave me a silly smile and slight nod before handing me the key to room 626.

I took the elevator to the sixth deck and walked down the passageway to my room. I went in and found it most pleasant. Although I didn't intend to spend much time there other than sleeping, it did have a relaxing atmosphere.

A nice double bed sat across from a dresser. At the east side of the room, French doors opened onto a small balcony with a waist-high, ornate, iron railing. Six decks down, the hotel swimming pool stretched 25 meters in length to the east. Several families and nubile young women surrounded it; a few of them intermittingly swam in its clear water.

I couldn't get over how clean everything was in contrast to the past 15 months—a time that remains a vision of filth. I thought of the rice paddies—with their fetid water, the vermin, the parasites, the blowing sand, and the red clay that stuck to you. One carried it as though it was part of the uniform. This, coupled with one's own sweat, gave you the feeling you permanently resided in a mud bath. Only now, after taking the second shower since arriving in Singapore did I realize how strange it was to feel clean for more than an hour.

I purchased a swim suit in one of the shops adjacent to the hotel and spent the remainder of the day around the pool, sampling the various brands of local and imported beers and attempting to converse with the lovelies. My haircut and scars gave me away; they must have known I made my living in Vietnam. They were reticent to talk to me— probably figured I was some kind of animal. I didn't care; I just drank beer.

Apparently I unwound more than I thought because I turned in at 1900, after grabbing a sandwich. The thought of sleeping with no fear of incoming rounds or the need to check night defensive positions let me drift into a sound and recuperative sleep.

Up at 0700, I'd bagged 12 hours in the pad. When I awoke, my body felt refreshed but weak. I suppose the absence of tension made it seem so.

It was Sunday morning, another bright and pleasant day. I dressed and went to the lobby and asked the young woman at the desk about the nearest Catholic Church and the time of Masses. She told me the Jesuit parish was about two miles distance. A simple route, I walked to the 0800 service.

I entered to find few people in the Gothic structure. One of the Jesuits heard my confession. I always liked them; they had both feet on the ground and understood life, along with man's frailties. Their pragmatic, intellectual and spiritual guidance helped keep my life in perspective.

A very old priest said Mass, and he shuffled about the altar with great difficulty. I wondered from where he came and if the shortage of priests since Vatican II required him to keep serving, even if in a limited capacity. I thought too of our Navy chaplains. Some suffered crises of faith and attempted to run away from whatever. Going to Vietnam didn't help their struggles. I felt sorry for one in particular. While trying to find himself, he took a round in the head. He lived, but it left him a vegetable.

My five days in Singapore gave me what I needed and wanted: time away from trauma. I went on tours and absorbed the island's history, particularly how the Japanese took it in World War II. The best part, I stayed away from anybody I knew, except for the last day.

Wednesday came too soon. I found it hard to think I would return to Vietnam the next morning.

That evening I went to the pool bar to enjoy my last night away from the war. Unusually crowded and noisy, most of the patrons had started earlier than I did.

Next to me stood an Australian, ordering a round of drinks for his mates at a nearby table. Right away he spotted me as an American before I'd said anything. Again, the haircut and I suppose my jaded look gave me away.

"Here from Nam?" he asked. I told him who I was and wondered about him. He introduced himself as Major Samuel Burns, a Royal Australian finance officer, and then he asked me to join his party.

I accepted and helped him carry the drinks to his table, where he proceeded to present me to his group.

High spirits ruled among the four other officers, three of whom had their wives with them. The ladies, all very attractive and subdued, nicely complemented their outgoing husbands.

I don't remember all of their names now, except for one: an English major they introduced as Spencer Cattley. He said he had spent 10 months as an exchange officer studying other countries' military pay systems. He'd visited the United States once—some place called Fort Harrison where the U.S. Army had its finance center. After studying the Australian system for two months, he would return to his Worthy Down office in England. The contingent had also taken a short trip to Singapore where I came to know him.

The Australians drank prodigious amounts of beer, and all the while they laughed and took indirect jabs at the British major. The more they drank the worse it got. Major Cattley didn't know how to handle it, which made it all the more humorous. Apparently he had attended some kind of gentlemanly protocol course, but he either missed the class on how to deal with colonials, or they didn't teach it.

Eventually, it became downright embarrassing as the evening progressed. Major Cattley noted my indifference to his dilemma, but he did try and change the subject by asking me about Vietnam. I told him I was here to forget about the place, not talk about it. The Australians laughed.

The flustered officer, his lips pulsating and his eyes bulging, tried to sip from the Rob Roy he'd artfully described, emphasizing the drink's sophistication to everyone earlier in the evening.

The prissy Major Cattley had obviously annoyed the earthy and tough Australians by his know-it-all attitude. They collectively released their contempt for this man they had, of necessity, treated properly in their own country. Once on neutral ground, however, they went after him.

I felt uncomfortable and actually sorry for the major. He was no soldier, and although out of his element, he didn't deserve the humiliation the Aussies heaped upon him. I suggested that we leave and grab a cup of espresso down the street at a nearby coffee shop. He agreed. We excused ourselves and headed out of the bar area, through the lobby and onto the main street.

A block from the hotel we came onto the coffee house and went inside. The bar was small. It had half a dozen tables and a counter with an equal number of stools facing it. Dark hardwoods graced both the deck and the bulkheads and gave off a pleasant ambiance. I suspected the wood represented valuable and exotic timber unique to the Asian region. I wanted to ask the proprietor about it, but instead just ordered a couple of espressos while the major took a seat at a corner table.

Before I could sit down, Major Cattley took on a manic air and began to talk hurriedly. He first thanked me for liberating him from the embarrassing position the Australians had placed him. As though saved from unspeakable agony, he must have seen me as both a savior and a friend. He began to confide in me and to vent as though a series of pent up emotions needed airing.

He told me how he missed his home base, his simple apartment and his uncomplicated lifestyle. He next told me he was a loner and that his salvation rested in his devotion to his career and his service to the Queen. Noting that he excelled in fiscal matters and all the details surrounding them, he proudly related that these traits enabled him to overshadow his less than stellar military appearance and be seen by his superiors as a most valuable asset to the British army. For these reasons, they sent him to exchange duty in the United States and on special assignments like the one to the Australian forces; however, he had grown weary and only wanted to return to England. I was beginning to hear more than I really wanted to know.

Like some officers I had branded, he wanted me to be aware of his importance. I wondered if this really masked a sense of insecurity.

I asked him what he did in his off hours and what hobbies he had. He said he liked to vacation in Spain a couple of times a year and would holiday on the Costa de Sol in the eastern part of the country. He said he went by himself.

At this point, his face took on a melancholy stare and a wave of sadness seemed to engulf him.

All the while I looked at him I knew Major Cattley as my true enemy. English and a soldier, he was little different from the blokes I had killed before escaping Ireland; however, he seemed so harmless, unarmed and pathetic. Dare I think of eliminating him too?

Suddenly he went from manic to melancholy and now back to manic. He shook off his depression and alighted upon a new line of conversation. He queried me about my background, my unit in Vietnam, my home, my relatives and a myriad of other things. I couldn't respond because he talked nonstop. Stuck on transmit, the guy spoke incessantly, all the while interjecting comments about his professionalism, his extraordinary attention to detail and his exceptional abilities.

He quickly became a bore. Fixated on himself, he must have felt he had a captive audience; one awed by his importance. I yawned, and he stopped talking.

Possibly he'd had too many Rob Roys because he shifted gears again and his voice became slightly belligerent. Sipping his espresso, his eyes took on a demonic facade. He then began to question my accent and asked if I had come from Ireland. He told me his extraordinary attention to detail focused on the subtleties of my verbiage, and that it appeared I had tried to mask my origins.

He continued this line without letting me answer by saying that he thought he knew me. I froze when he said, "You're Ned O'Shea, the bloody IRA bastard raised by nuns in a Wexford orphanage and on the wanted list!"

Major Cattley apprised me that I became suspicious to him all evening because he thought he'd seen my picture before…a disheveled appearance with unruly hair and a beard. It appeared on a wanted poster for an IRA operative.

I told him he was full of shit and started to leave. He said he wanted to accompany me back to the hotel. I said nothing and left, but in a flash he was right beside me, telling me he had political connections and that he could unmask my guise unless we made a deal. I asked what kind of deal, to which he gave me his room number and invited me up if I wanted to discuss it further. He then sprinted ahead of me and disappeared in the vicinity of the hotel.

I returned to my room somewhat ill-at-ease. I sat in the dark overlooking my balcony and gazing down at the lighted pool beneath me. A few folks swam, one doing laps and the others just milling around in the water.

I wondered what Cattley intended to do with the discovery he had made about me. Would he contact the US Embassy; go through his military channels; affect liaison with US military representatives in Singapore, or what? He told me to come to his room if I wanted to discuss it further. I reluctantly decided to do so.

About midnight I called his room. He answered, and I advised him I wanted to speak with him. He told me to come up. He would leave the door unlocked and to just enter on my own accord.

I slipped out of my room and went to Major Cattley's three floors up, entering as he had directed me.

He had no lights on, just like I had in my room. He sat in a chair with his back to the open balcony. He wore a silken robe and nursed a Rob Roy with aplomb. Although difficult to detect, it appeared he nurtured a Cheshire cat grin on his thin lips. He told me to sit in the chair opposite him and then asked what concerned me.

I told him I wanted to know what he intended to do with the information he thought he had on me. Without changing his expression he said it depended if we could make a deal. Make a deal? I had no idea where he intended to go with this, so I asked him what he meant. He rose from his chair, moved to the door opening to the balcony, then turned and faced me. His words had a tone of assurance and authority. "I want money," he said. "You're blackmailing me," I retorted. He assured me he was and that if I didn't comply, he would by message alert appropriate authorities, both English and American of both my fraud and my wanted status.

I sat in stunned silence for a moment and then asked how much money he wanted. He told me $10,000 American dollars. I told him I didn't have that much money and that at best all I could do was provide maybe half that.

He probably anticipated this response and said that he would provide me with instructions as to how I would forward monies to his secret Swiss bank account.

Major Cattley then made a fatal error. He conditioned his acceptance of this lesser amount of money if I would oblige him in another arena. He said he found me rather appealing and that he wanted to take our new relationship to another level.

That comment provided the last piece to the puzzle about this guy. It instantly came to me that I was told McGinty had betrayed the IRA cause through a gay English army finance officer and that our side had blackmailed him. He in turn said he had wanted money in return for exposing McGinty. And here I was standing face-to-face with this man who had just propositioned me.

What happened next was instantaneous. The anger and revulsion of the whole incident overwhelmed me. I shot out of my chair and in a crouched position sprang upward and with the heel of my right hand I caught the major flush on the chin; his body stiffened while at the same time he flew backwards towards the balcony railing. He flipped over it and fell with a thud in the alley below.

I peered down at his contorted body. His head angled off his torso in a menacing fashion; the fall had broken his neck. Cattley was dead.

Moving quickly to the door, I opened it and wiped the handles with my handkerchief and took the stairs to my room where I quickly packed and exited the hotel by a side entrance.

I walked several blocks and hailed a cab and had the cabbie take me to the R&R Center. I checked in and waited for the flight back to Vietnam. As it became light, men started to straggle in, wearing signs of exhaustion from sex, drinking and lack of sleep. At the designated time, we boarded the aircraft and lifted off the runway for our return to the horrors of war. No one said much. Everyone kept his own counsel and his premonitions of what awaited him.

I wondered about Major Cattley and what the authorities might be doing regarding his death. I suspected they could make me a party to their investigation if they thought it other than an accident or a suicide. Would they try and track me to Vietnam with no solid evidence that I had anything to do with it? Probably not...at least that is what I hoped.

CHAPTER 14

Our plane, the same one that brought us, would take us back to Vietnam and return with another R&R load. They'd screw the same broads and puke in the same passageways...an identical act, only the players would change.

We lifted off, wheels up at 0900 and watched Singapore fade into the distance. Each man wondered why he had to leave civilization and return to the terror and barbarism of war.

I didn't share their feelings. My preoccupation remained with the chance encounter with Major Cattley and my lucky exit from Singapore.

I hadn't intended to put my actual identity in these ramblings, but the Singapore incident changed that. Why deny the truth? Besides, nothing really matters that much anymore...possibly because I have this presage of death. It's near and haunting, like a nightmare from which I cannot awake. As busy as I remain, it's always there.

Only the Grim Reaper will select my death's composition. In the interim, he taunts his victims and causes us to wonder if his visit will be violent, or peaceful; will we be alone or among friends? Whichever, the call will surely come.

As our plane winged north, I tried to focus my thoughts away from death. They went back to Ireland and an IRA strategy meeting at an abandoned monastery. IRA leaders met to plan the army's next moves, and they'd included me in their plan. Yes, they had picked me to assassinate Queen Elizabeth when she visited a horse farm.

Within a week after I crossed the border into Northern Ireland, the big plan came apart.

They had me billeted in a seedy flat while I awaited further direction. A Sean McGinty, an IRA logistics chief, oversaw my stay in Northern Ireland. The first night I stayed in his home. He left to take care of some business, and while he was gone, his wife propositioned me.

Shortly after I moved into the flat, IRA operatives notified our group to return to the monastery for an unscheduled meeting. When we arrived, there was a new face in the crowd. He let everyone know that our plan had been compromised and the informant was McGinty. He was on the take from the British Army. They paid him to keep them apprised of our activities.

What followed wasn't pretty. McGinty pulled a knife on one of the IRA members, but before he did anything, I shot him from under the table—blew his knee cap away.

When he fell to the deck, everyone descended on him like a pack of wolves and beat him. He confessed to his activities before one of the assembled executed him...put a bullet in his head. We buried the fool on the island, without fanfare.

Poor McGinty—what people do for money. He had a wife and two children. Either greed or the want to better support his family made him sell the cause. Such a pity.

The British authorities had me as a marked man from that point, complete with photograph. Fortunately, the IRA had a contingency plan and had made arrangements to spirit me out of the country. I sailed from the port city of Cork on a Polish freighter bound for the United States.

Thomas Larkin helped me through the whole process, and I owe him much.

I liked Thomas Larkin. He treated me well and went out of his way to be kind and considerate. Maybe he did it because of my past, where such virtues seemed in short supply.

When I attended university, I went to Thurles in County Tipperary with a classmate. We stayed at his parent's home. I remember the affection they heaped on their son (unusual among the Irish), and how I'd never known such warmth. I envied him and long after wondered if such outward manifestations of closeness might have made me something other than what I am. I kill with indifference, without feeling. It's methodical and exact...and almost natural. And it never bothers me. Should it?

Thomas gave me the name of a Jerry O'Bannon in Boston. Jerry ran an underground network to help Irish immigrants entering the country illegally. He placed them in various low visibility jobs.

As if I hadn't experienced enough disappointment, while sailing aboard the Polish freighter I came face to face with my father who had abandoned me as a child. The worthless tool reeked of hedonism. Totally self-serving, I shot the son-of-a-bitch one night on the fantail of the ship using the same pistol I shot McGinty with, and then pushed him over the fantail into the wake of the ship.

When I finally reached the United States, the nation seemed at odds with itself. The Vietnam War, in full swing, had many perplexed. I realized this one night, after walking around downtown Boston. I stopped at a small pub; I had only enough money for a beer.

Sitting at the bar, I ordered a Harp and took a nostalgic sip, feeling homesick for Ireland.

Next to me sat a ruddy faced man with a stern expression. He reminded me of someone with high blood pressure. Unable to contain himself, he asked if I'd served in Vietnam. I told him I hadn't and tried to play the role of a college student.

Been drafted yet?" he asked.

"No, not yet, but I suspect I will when I finish school."

He continued, "You don't sound like Boston Irish; did you just arrive from the old sod or something?"

"I've been here awhile," I said as I tried to mask my brogue.

"Have you thought about which armed service you'd like to join?"

"I really haven't; school's had me a bit busy lately."

"Want some advice?" he snorted.

I could tell he'd been drinking heavily and appeared to have some kind of emotional baggage tugging at him.

"I'm listening," I said in an indifferent tone.

He hesitated a moment, looking like he wasn't sure if I was mocking him or if I really wanted him to render counsel.

"Join the Marine Corps," he said as he turned back to the bar. He then took a swig from his mug and lowered his head.

"Why the Marine Corps, friend?"

"Because it's the only place in this fucked-up country where you'll find anything resembling the truth. There isn't any bullshit in the Corps. They put all the cards on the table all the time."

"I take it you served in the Marine Corps...I didn't get your name."

"It's Joseph Cassidy, First Sergeant, United States Marine Corps, Retired.

And yes, I did serve the Corps for 26 years. I fought in World War II, the Korean War and put one tour in 'Nam, 1965. I lost a leg there, and the Navy medically discharged me. So here I sit, watching your fucked-up generation turn coward. At times I'm ashamed to call myself an American."

He went back to his beer, and he never looked at me again.

Uncomfortably, I finished my Harp and said, "Thanks for the advice First Sergeant. I'll take it under advisement." Little did I know how sage it was.

CHAPTER 15

Things moved quickly after my chance encounter with First Sergeant Cassidy. Jerry O'Bannon contacted me two days later. I'd hoped that he'd found some rich Bostonian who'd hire an illegal alien and would not report any wages to the IRS.

Jerry spoke in animated terms. "Ned, I've found a place for you."

"That's good news, Jerry."

"Well Ned, this is a bit unusual, but I think it's a good match. I received word of a Boston College graduate student who'd just received his draft notice, and he's scheduled to report for induction early next month.

"According to my reports, he's going to dodge the draft and live in Canada; however, what he'd really like to do is stay in school...somewhere."

"What's that got to do with me, Jerry?"

"It's easy, Ned. You'll assume his identification and replace him in the draft, serve a couple of years in the Army, and he'll continue in school. You'll both make out that way."

I wasn't so sure.

"Wait a minute, Jerry. This country is at war. It's a pretty lousy trade if you ask me. Besides, I'm not looking to have me butt all shot away."

Jerry looked at me pensively and sighed. "Ned, things are drying up. I'm having a hard time keeping you guys moving and away from the immigration authorities. They caught two of you lads this week, and I'm afraid someone will unmask our covert efforts.

"Ned, what I'm saying is that little option remains for you. You'll have to act on this or possibly the police will nab you. They extradited one fellow, Joe Curran, to Northern Ireland because of crimes he'd committed there.

"I don't know if you're harboring any misdeeds, but we need to move quickly."

"You don't give me much choice, Jerry; guess I'll have to defer to your judgment. What's my next move?"

"I'll arrange a meeting with your double. He can pass all identifying data to you. You'll study them and then report for induction, unless..."

"Come on Jerry—cut the crap and put the cards on the table!"

"Well Ned, you see we have a few military recruiters in Boston who need to make their monthly quotas. They ask no questions, and we feed them men from time to time. Chief Petty Officer Randall and Gunnery Sergeant Milton are hurting. It's the end of the month, and they're short—so you have an option, Ned. You can volunteer for either the

Navy or the Marines; otherwise, the Army will draft you. The Air Force is full up for the next two months.

Without hesitation, I told Jerry I'd go in the Marine Corps. I was proficient with small arms and figured I might feel more at home there than on a ship. Ten days on the Polish freighter convinced me I'd do better on land. Besides, First Sergeant Cassidy's endorsement, even though a bit blunt, rang true. It sounded like a place I would fit.

The next evening I met the man I would replace in the draft. His name became mine—Thomas Kagan. The guy wasn't just an asshole; he was a flaming asshole. He had beady eyes, a very stupid looking beard and long greasy hair. His pus-ridden complexion made me feel like I was visiting a leper colony. I almost suggested he wear a bell around his neck.

Jerry O'Bannon made the introductions and sort of acted like the arbitrator in our deal. He knew right off I didn't like the specious, condescending bastard. He acted like he was doing me a favor, all the while bad mouthing his country and the "stupid military." I struggled to hold my contempt in check.

I walked out of Jerry's office with a portfolio containing the induction notice, Kagan's birth certificate, his Social Security card, college transcripts, and a myriad of other data to support the false identification. That night I studied it intently, and the next morning I called Gunnery Sergeant Milton.

Jerry O'Bannon had already told Gunny Milton about me. He'd also provided him all the administrative information he needed on Kagan. So, when I called his office, he said he'd already processed my enlistment contract. He then cheerfully added that all I needed to do was pass the physical examination, and he'd put me on a bus to Parris Island, South Carolina for boot camp.

I passed the physical.

What followed consisted of roughly 11 months of what some might call hell. Actually, as I look back, I thrived in the environment. I liked challenges and many would lie in front of me.

One could write volumes on Marine Corps boot camp, the Officer Candidate Course, and the follow-on Basic School for commissioned officers. I think the period truly molded me. The Irish Republican Army hadn't totally prepared me for what the Marine Corps demanded. Functioning alone wasn't the name of the Marine Corps game.

The grueling weeks of training turned into months as my body hardened, and I took on a new discipline and pride.

A real break came when my recruit platoon went to the rifle range. Up to that point, I'd tried to maintain a low profile, and to stay out of trouble and not do anything that might jeopardize my assumed status as Thomas Kagan.

I'd made it through Recruit Receiving, taking a battery of tests and getting my clothing, bucket and rifle issue. We drilled, underwent intense physical training, attended numerous classes and weeks later reported to the Weapons Training Battalion for rifle qualification. Here I felt at home. We used the M-14 rifle; it fired the 7.62 NATO round. It had ballistics similar to the .30 caliber I used with the IRA, although not as good. It had a slightly lower muzzle velocity, similar to the British .303.

The American military had tried to create an all-purpose weapon with the M-14. It would fire either semi-automatic or full-automatic, but it lost something in the process—balance. Heavy and awkward, it felt clumsy compared to the M-1 Garand the IRA gave me.

Regardless, marksmanship principles remain the same, and I knew I could master the weapon, no matter how difficult it was to fire.

After zeroing it, I began to hone the skills I'd developed months previously on Irish beaches.

The skills jelled by qualification day.

I fired in the first relay, and when we started at the 200 yard line, the range flag hung flaccid...no wind. As I cranked in the exact dope on my rifle sights, I felt confident and determined.

It was no fluke. I put round after round in the bulls eye. Through rapid fire, through the 300 yard mark and finally the 500 yard line—I continued to blast the target. When our relay finished, I had fired a 248 out of a possible 250 points on the marksmanship course.

Word filtered up about the recruit who had burned up the course. Soon the battalion commander called for me. I stood rigid in front of his desk. He complimented me on my performance and related that my marksmanship score was another indicator of how well I'd done thus far. He said the Weapons Training Battalion wanted me to remain after graduation to become an instructor. He had other ideas.

My university degree, high General Classification Test score and good performance in all phases of recruit training made him think I should go to Quantico and train to become an officer. I had no objections.

One observation about boot camp and my initial exposure to the Marine Corps: A strange, informal means of communication existed within its structure. I realized that the formality of command did not control everything.

I mention this because of one incident that had a strong impact on me. Our drill instructor (DI) was a Staff Sergeant by the name of Harden. He was the meanest man I have ever met. I never saw him smile or pay anyone a compliment. No one ever did anything right.

Our company commander was a Captain Taylor. He served a tour of duty in Korea instead of Vietnam, came to Parris Island for a short tour and had orders to the Marine Barracks, Boston.

He annoyed Staff Sergeant Harden, because whenever he was in the area, he would point to anything adrift and say, "What's that?"

This went on the whole period of our training.

I didn't realize how much the captain's actions bothered our DI until we were scheduled for our final inspection, two days before we graduated from boot camp, and right before Captain Taylor left for Boston.

Harden directed me to sanitize one commode in our head.

I scoured it out, sprinkled bowl cleaner in it and put tape over it with a sign saying "Do Not Use." Then I had to stand guard over it.

The day before the big inspection, Harden wanted to know if anyone in the platoon had studied sculpture.

One recruit, Christopher Dasher, said he had a fine arts degree.

Harden then handed him a jar of peanut butter and directed him to sculpt a piece of human fecal matter.

Dasher spent the better part of one afternoon obliging Harden.

When he presented his finished product, I saw Harden's eyes light up.

He told Dasher to tactically place it in the commode I guarded. That night, I continued to stand guard over the commode. No one was to disturb the piece of art.

At 0900 the next morning, Captain Taylor conducted his inspection of our barracks.

He didn't change his routine, but went about saying "What's that?"

Finally, he entered the head.

Harden was to his immediate left.

He came by the sanitized commode with the work of art in it and said "What's that?"

Harden immediately reached into the bowl and scooped up a large portion of the peanut butter onto his right index finger.

He put the finger into his mouth and said..."Sir, that's fecal matter, sir!"

Captain Taylor wheeled about and left the area.

We never saw him again, and I think I might have detected a suppressed smile on the corners of Staff Sergeant Harden's mouth.

Everything fell into place after recruit graduation. The Corps shipped me off to Quantico, Virginia where I went through a compressed boot camp—same type of subjects, only everything seemed more intense and expanded.

The Marine Corps commissioned me a second lieutenant in the spring of 1967, and I moved from the main side officer candidate area to Camp Barrett, home of the officer "Basic School."

The Vietnam War made many demands on the Corps, so it had shortened the officers' course from eight to six months to put more of us out quicker. Again, during a compressed and intense period, the Corps taught me to lead as a company grade officer. The training was superb.

Our company graduated in November. Shortly before then, I received my designated Military Occupational Specialty—0302; I would be an infantry officer. I received my orders, too. I would report to Travis Air Force Base within 45 days and proceed on a designated Military Airlift Command flight to the Republic of Vietnam for duty with the storied 1st Marine Division. The orders didn't surprise me.

Many in my company had orders to Vietnam too. A few went to the 2d Marine Division at Camp Lejeune, North Carolina, some to flight school, and others to artillery school, but most of us went to WESTPAC.

Some of my classmates asked if I would take leave in Boston before shipping out. I said I wasn't sure, but I knew otherwise. I would avoid Boston for obvious reasons.

Upon graduation, I rented a car and drove west. I swung south because of the coming winter and ambled across the United States, to places I'd only read about in books.

Awed by the majesty and vastness of the land, only one thing struck me outside its greatness: The people seemed bemused by the war. Although I'd heard nothing but war for the last year, I couldn't help but observe in town after town that life seemed normal. No one evidenced any awareness or care about the US commitment to Vietnam. It confused me. Here was a nation at war, yet it acted like nothing unusual was happening. Unless they had a relative involved, the average citizens kept on about their business. They suffered no shortages or inconveniences.

I reached the California coast with seven days left on my leave. I took my time as I drove north. I stayed in small, coastal towns and walked the beaches in the early mornings and late evenings.

I did a lot of reading on the trip—books by Bernard Fall on Vietnam and other authors recording the troubled times in Southeast Asia. I also read a short history of the First Marine Division, to which I was headed. It consisted of three infantry regiments, the 1st, 5th and 7th. Elements of it had gained fame in the trenches during World War I, and it expanded during World War II fighting for control of strange sounding islands like Guadalcanal and Peleliu making an indelible mark on American society. It followed on to Korea where it built continued prominence in battles like Inchon and the Chosin Reservoir. I wondered as I paged through its annals if it had retained its esprit de corps in the new environs of Vietnam and if its leaders measured up to its past stalwart commanders. And I wondered too why my life had become so complex. When I graduated from college, I had no idea that things would go the direction they had.

I hated to see my trip end, but it did. I turned in my rental car in San Francisco and caught a bus to Travis Air Force Base. I met 14 of my Basic School platoon classmates there, all waiting for the same flight that would take us to Vietnam. Some were pensive; others were talkative. Three married while on leave and had their wives with them at Travis, trying to extend their honeymoons as long as possible. Among the 15 of us, all infantry, five would die in the next year and eight would be wounded.

When the magic hour arrived, we dutifully boarded our plane and began the long flight into hardship and terror.

CHAPTER 16

Deja vu: A sense of alarm returned as our plane approached the Vietnam coast and vectored to its assigned position in Da Nang's landing pattern. The partially overcast sky and the smoke rising from fetid points of land, gave the impression Vietnam was one huge garbage dump.

I felt disparaged as the plane flared on final and the wheels protested their sudden contact with the runway.

Maneuvering his aircraft to the military terminal, the pilot shut down the engines and a stewardess opened the rear hatch.

A gust of furnace like air rushed into the plane's interior and beads of perspiration quickly formed on everyone's brow. Grimly, we took our few belongings and filed down the awaiting ramp.

No one else from my company had gone to Singapore for R&R. Two others from various units within the battalion did, and we all followed signs directing us to a pickup point for our trip back north.

We changed back into our combat gear and within the hour, boarded a truck. The driver skirted Da Nang, ending up at the Marble Mountain airstrip adjacent to the South China Sea. Here we embarked on a resupply chopper making a run to our battalion in Quang Tri Province. My watch read 1700.

As we churned north, I wondered how my platoon had fared the past week; who the new company executive officer might be; if we were in the same positions or had moved elsewhere in the region; was Charlie quiet or up to no good.

Evening shadows began to appear when the bird set down on the battalion resupply pad.

We hustled off the aircraft and went our separate ways. Corporal Warton, our company supply clerk, had the company jeep and trailer standing by to pick up ammo, rations and myself.

"Welcome back, lieutenant," he said quietly.

The subdued tone of his voice sounded like that of a funeral director. I sensed something wrong, but said nothing.

I climbed into the right front seat, and we headed to the company's position.

"We really got into some bad shit while you were gone, Lieutenant Kagan."

"What happened?" I asked, resigned to the worst.

"Three nights ago, Charlie hit us big time. Word is a NVA battalion did the work. We had 13 KIAs in the company and 35 WIAs; it was really bad, sir.

"Your platoon seemed to catch the brunt of the attack— seven KIAs and 15 WIAs."

My stomach knotted, and I felt guilty about my absence.

"The worst of it, lieutenant, is that the captain, Lieutenants Cook and O'Brien, and First Sergeant Christensen all died in the attack. Staff Sergeant LaCount got it too."

I sat stunned, like someone had just loaded me with a double dose of morphine. I couldn't believe what I heard. These selfless and good men, who had become so much a part of my life, were now gone. I thought of Staff Sergeant LaCount's family preparing for his homecoming next month, and how word of his death would shatter their lives and leave them so alone in an unconcerned nation.

The deaths in Northern Ireland made sense. These didn't.

"We got a new skipper, sir, and a new executive officer too. They arrived yesterday from division headquarters.

"Morale has hit rock bottom, lieutenant," Corporal Warton concluded.

We pulled into the company area, and I bailed out of the jeep and started for my platoon.

About halfway there, Lieutenant Morely called to me and came running over from his platoon's position.

"Tom, am I glad to see you. Things really turned sour after you left. The old man got killed, along with Arthur Cook, Ken O'Brien and a bunch of others."

"Yeah, Corporal Warton told me on the way from the helo pad."

"Then you know about Staff Sergeant LaCount too?"

"Yes, I do."

I could tell Fred bordered on the ragged edge. Nervous and agitated, his unseeing eyes spasmodically darted back and forth. Stretched to the limit, he needed to talk. We sat on a couple of 60mm ammo boxes and sipped tepid black coffee from our canteen cups while Fred spoke incessantly.

Sometimes, after the first real contact with the enemy, a person settles down, and the anticipation and associated apprehension of battle passes. This didn't seem to happen with Fred Morely. The death of Captain Klein and the two other platoon commanders unnerved him. He told me how the battalion 81mm mortar platoon put up a steady stream of illumination rounds when Charlie hit. He happened to look back toward the company command post to see Captain Klein, Lieutenant O'Brien and the First Sergeant all outlined against the night sky. Then a Rocket Propelled Grenade (RPG-7) or 82mm mortar hit right in the middle of them. He ran to help, but the round had killed them all. The company gunnery sergeant sustained severe wounds.

Arthur Cook assumed command of the company, only to suffer the same fate 10 minutes later, this time from AK-47 rounds.

Fortunately, the company had its defensive fires in place and the interlocking bands of chest high fire cut down Charlie's night attack when it hit the wire. They breached it in front of my platoon, but the intense fires drove them back as they tried to carry their dead and wounded with them. Even so, the men found 41 bodies the next morning.

Then Fred went off on a tangent, saying he hadn't heard from his wife for three weeks. In her last letter she told him she couldn't stand the separation and that she needed some diversion. She also said her type couldn't spend the nights sitting on her hands.

"I think she's having an affair, Tom!"

His wild eyes and quivering mouth startled me for a moment, as he tried to drink from his canteen cup. He shook like a man afflicted with Parkinson's disease.

"And to make matters worse," he went on, "the new company commander is some kind of a political dandy fellow. He said we took the casualties we did because the company was fucked up and the division commander had personally picked him to straighten it out. He was the general's aide, and he brought the assistant aide as his executive officer. He's a clone of the company commander; it's tweedledum and tweedledee! It is they against us!

"I hate this rotten place. I hate this stupid war. I hate it all!"

Fred dropped his canteen cup between his feet and began to sob, burying his face in his hands.

We sat there silently for a couple of minutes. Finally I told Fred to stay put, and that I'd return in a few minutes.

I walked a couple of hundred meters back to the battalion aid station. Doctor Dick Costa, our unflappable battalion surgeon, rested on a stretcher that was raised on a couple of sawhorses, reading a dime store western by the light of a kerosene lantern.

"Hi, Tom; how did R&R go? Why the glum face? You didn't come down with some incurable disease did you?" Doctor Costa had trouble taking anything too seriously.

"Sir, I wonder if you would come over by my platoon. I have Lieutenant Morely there, and I think he needs help, maybe a shot of that medicinal bourbon or something stronger. He's pretty upset about recent events and seems overwhelmed."

"I trust your judgment, Tom. We'll have a look."

Together we walked to Fred's side. Although silent, he remained with his face in his hands.

"Fred, Doctor Costa wants to talk with you. I'm going to check on my men. Take care. I'll see you later."

I never saw him again. Doctor Costa medevaced him to the USS Repose that night. He told me the next morning he thought Fred had some deep-seated emotional problems and that he probably needed extended care. The stress of combat apparently brought them to the surface. I felt badly for him.

I spent the day trying to pull together what I had left of a platoon. The casualties reduced my unit strength to little more than a couple of reinforced squads. The men, shaken and gaunt-eyed, had that 1,000 meter stare...not a good sign.

My right guide, Sergeant Gilmore, had taken over as platoon sergeant. Although tough, like Staff Sergeant

LaCount, he displayed a more laid back approach. Half of the remaining men had served in country for less than two months. Replacements would consist mainly of new men or rejects from other units: a chance for them to dump their trash.

At about 0930, the company runner came to our position and said the company commander wanted to see me right away. I told the runner I'd be along shortly.

I pulled on my utility jacket and my pistol belt and walked the 100 meters to the company CP. As I approached the new CO's bunker, I saw two men standing outside it. One, a tall man with legs apart and hands on his hips, stared at me as I approached. The other, a smaller figure to his left rear, struck a similar pose. Could these be tweedledum and tweedledee as Fred described them?

They both wore shoulder holsters, authorized only for tracked vehicle Marines. Their comfort and ease of wear made them favorites among certain heavies at division level. I guess the two of them wanted to impress everyone with their previous and continued importance. The new captain looked like he'd stepped out of a fashion magazine. A handsome man, over six feet tall with blond hair, he wore a starched and meticulously ironed utility uniform. He had shined boots and a fresh haircut.

"Lieutenant Kagan reporting as ordered, sir," I said.

The captain glared down at me like I was some kind of nondescript piece of fecal matter.

"Aren't you forgetting something, lieutenant?" he said, as the one corner of his upper lip raised in a snarl of disgust.

"No sir, I'm not," came my direct answer.

"Why didn't you salute?" he said with equal directness.

"Because I didn't want some NVA sniper to pick you off, sir. This happens to be a combat zone, and battalion policy directs that we don't salute under such conditions."

His eyes widened and a momentary look of foolishness crossed his face. He realized his rear echelon protocol didn't fit anymore than his fastidious appearance.

Annoyed by his obvious ineptness and inexperience in the combat world, he went into the attack mode to reassert his authority.

"I heard this morning from the battalion commander, Lieutenant Colonel Flaherty, that I'm down to one platoon commander and that's you. Why didn't you contact me before you went directly to the battalion surgeon with Lieutenant Morely's problem? That's the last time you bypass me on anything, lieutenant! I don't like surprises, nor is anyone going to upstage me. Do you understand?"

I looked in disbelief at this comical excuse for a company commander. Raving like some PMS-charged woman, the simpleton was trying to pull the drill instructor routine on me. Totally unprofessional in his rapport, I knew right away the company had in command a political animal, not a Marine Corps officer.

"I would hate to think captain that every time I have a wounded or sick man I'd have to call 'captain' instead of 'corpsman.' Secondly, sir, I didn't intentionally bypass you. I didn't even know you. I hadn't met you until just now.

"Don't get smart with me, lieutenant."

"I'm not, sir. You asked a question and I gave you an honest answer."

"You heard the captain," came a high pitched rejoinder from the new executive officer. He, unlike the captain, stood about five foot seven and had dark hair and eyes. His utility uniform had the same tailored appearance as did the commanding officer's.

"Listen dope, I've had more rain run off my poncho than you have time in front of troops, so don't play any seniority games with me. I'd ask you to visit my platoon, but I'm afraid you might dirty your boots. When you've earned everyone's respect, you can start asserting yourself. Until then, you'd best maintain a low profile," I said as I turned back to the captain.

"That's enough of that salty talk, Lieutenant Kagan," came the captain's response. He knew I'd directed my words at him as much as I did to his executive officer.

A strained silence overtook the three of us. We stood, realizing a common purpose, yet viewing it in such different ways.

Our new company commander, 28 years-old Captain Lester Parker, represented the system, just as I did. We'd both received the same training, but it ended there. I was a mud Marine whereas Captain Parker favored political contacts to further his career. He'd held high visibility staff jobs for a company grade officer and, in his mind, had achieved some recognition within the Corps. But a serious impairment plagued him: he put his own ambition above the unit's mission and the men. The captain's superiors didn't readily see this, but his subordinates did. And they would not trust him because of his blinding ambition. They would see themselves as his tools, something he would use and then discard. He took subordinates for granted, and saw them in the light of only what they might do for him.

I'd dismissed the executive officer, 1st Lieutenant Charles Stewart, as nothing more than a Hollywood stand in. Aping Captain Parker, he neither grasped tactics nor his position within the company; I think he'd forgotten everything they'd taught at the Basic School. He thought the only contribution he need make was to follow the captain around and proscribe innocuous happenings. Like Captain Taylor at Parris Island, he played the minutiae game, becoming an itch to all hands, and needlessly tormenting those who deserved no such antics. And to add to this facade, he patronized Captain Parker ad nauseam; however, the insecure captain thrived on it.

After Captain Parker had berated me for seeking medical help for Fred Morely, I came to attention and smartly saluted him, while a sardonic grin strained at the corners of my mouth.

The captain didn't know whether to return the salute or walk away. He did neither but simply glared at me. He suspected I'd mocked his lack of combat experience and had invited his early demise.

I dropped my salute, executed an about face and marched back to my platoon. I'd seen too much to respond to the silly head games the new commanding officer was playing in an attempt to establish his authority. He failed to appreciate that everyone knew he had the responsibility of command; no one questioned his authority.

CHAPTER 17

Captain Parker made the following days difficult, not in a physical sense, but in his bizarre approach to command. Everything he did appeared political—an orchestrated attempt to make him look good. Whenever the company didn't perform to expectations, he'd attempt to blame someone else. Rather than be accountable, he looked for ways to cover up discrepancies, even if it meant falsifying official records. His executive officer, Lieutenant Stewart, saw the impropriety of these acts, but he distanced himself from them and did nothing to counteract Captain Parker's trickery.

Three green second lieutenants joined the company within the month to replace the platoon leaders we'd lost.

We also acquired a new company first sergeant and gunnery sergeant. The gunny, on his second tour, is salty and professional in every sense.

The first sergeant, Barton Gunther, on the other hand is stupid beyond belief and disloyal too. The ranks of the Marine Corps have expanded, and this has accelerated promotions. He is one of those who slipped through the crack;

at peace-time manning levels, promotion boards would have never picked him. I believe management experts call it "adverse selection."

He makes it a point to pull his time in service on the new lieutenants, informing Captain Parker of their lack of experience and abilities. Instead of putting the first sergeant in his place, the captain encourages this behavior so as to keep his officers at bay and unsure of his support. At various times, all three of the new lieutenants have come to me in frustration, their morale down. Each feels that disaster awaits us.

I encourage them to stay the course. My limited experience has taught me that the Corps and its system of command is sound, and that eventually its leaders will correct a bad situation. But I worry...does the battalion commander see through Captain Parker, or is he the anointed one? Whatever, we have to remain loyal, even though he isn't.

It all came into perspective when the captain spoke one evening after we'd set in our night defensive positions and turned in our map overlays at the company command post.

Under the influence of alcohol, he waxed eloquently on his VMI education. He was very proud of his affiliation with the institution and let us know that it generated such tenacious leaders as Confederate General Thomas J. "Stonewall" Jackson, Army Generals George Patton and George Marshall and Marine General Lem Sheperd.

He took particular pains to tell us about the Virginia Military Institute Corps of Cadets at the battle of New

Market, Virginia on May 15, 1864. They carried the day as 4,500 Confederates under General John C. Breckinridge defeated a Federal force of 6,500.

Captain Parker further elaborated that on May 15th, VMI commemorates that great victory with a very moving ceremony. At roll call, as the names of the New Market casualties are called, hand-picked cadets bark their replies, "Dead on the field of honor, sir!" Of course, Captain Parker was always one of the selected cadets.

He should have stopped there, but he didn't.

He apprised us that his uncle, Senator John Bucknole, influenced his assignment as a White House Fellow and later as General Walker's aide. Now he needed command time to enhance his career before he rotated back to the States. Thus, we learned the real reason he took over Golf Company. He said he intends to win at least a Navy Cross, keeping him on the fast track to make general officer.

The other platoon commanders looked at each other with incredulous expressions. And myself? I lowered my head and spit between my legs. It's one thing to think such thoughts, but something else again to express them. All the while Lieutenant Stewart stood behind Captain Parker with a fixed grin, nodding at everything he said—what a vegetable.

The captain, too caught up with himself to realize his captive audience viewed him as a buffoon, continued to speak. What he said next made more sense than anything he'd expressed before.

He reflected on history and each of our places in it, and opined that some men have risen to greatness only because of the times in which they lived. They had but one chance to capture a certain moment in world events. We, for example, would never fight again as company grade officers. Maybe in our lifetimes there would be another war, but we would never serve in the capacity we are now.

It followed then in Captain Parker's mind that one had to make the best of his time at hand. There would be but one chance for each of us to do that. Marshall, Patton and Sheperd did, as did von Manstein, Rommel, Forrest, Grant, Jackson and Lee. They achieved greatness because they responded to their particular moment in history. Others lived in the same period but either didn't have the abilities or the drive to succeed.

He then went back on his ego trip and how this was "his" moment in history and come hell or high water, he would achieve greatness! He smiled sinisterly and then launched into stories about the women he'd made. Even though married, he wanted all of us to know what a real stud he was and how his multiple conquests qualified him for some sort of record. His type usually never made it to first base with anyone other than a prostitute, and he probably got VD in the process. What a bore. Even his executive officer became uneasy with his tasteless ramblings.

I could take no more, so I stood up and returned to my platoon, not saying a word or looking back to see if he disapproved of my abrupt departure. About twenty meters from his position, I heard talking behind me. The other platoon commanders had taken my cue and started for their platoons too, having followed my lead from the insanity.

At that moment we heard the belligerent voice of Captain Parker call from his bunker, "You fucking pricks! I'll have every one of you worthless bastards—you so called leaders. If not for me, you'd all be fucking dead because I'm the greatest captain and leader of our times."

I turned to see the drunken image of Captain Parker urinating at the entrance to his bunker.

The next morning, about 0830, the company runner came to my position and said the captain wanted me right away...something about a platoon mission. I followed the young Marine back to Captain Parker's bunker. I entered to see him sitting behind his field desk, eyes bloodshot and a look of complete contempt on his swollen and gin-sodden face. He must have felt terrible, but he had vengeance in his eyes.

He made no mention of his conduct the previous night, but advised me to saddle up my platoon and reconnoiter three thousand meters to the company's front and not return for two days.

"What am I looking for, sir?" I asked.

"For the fucking enemy—the only one we've got, asshole!" he blurted out, not even trying to control his anger.

"I figured that, captain, but do we have some hard intelligence on exactly the type of enemy? Are they VC or

NVA? What's their size and armament? And further, what about resupply? Do you have a radio for me and what frequencies do I need for air and artillery support and medevacs? Do you have a map overlay of the route you want me to take?"

He cut me off before I could ask another question. It was obvious he hadn't thought of any of these things, but had rather hatched this harebrained scheme to get even for my perceived disrespect. I doubted that battalion headquarters even knew what he had planned.

"Get the fuck out of my bunker, lieutenant!"

I'd made no attempt to make him look incompetent, but I had to protect the so-called "mission," and my men too. Captain Parker had no vision of what we were about. He focused only on head games. He was simply obsessed with trying to ensure that everyone viewed him as the king. The war remained only on the periphery of his mind. As I came to realize this, I slowly began to share the other officers' sense of our impending destruction.

I left without saying anything. As I walked back to my platoon, I wondered how a company as good as ours could change so quickly—but it had. Our new skipper is a nut case.

Today I brooded. I wanted to be alone with my thoughts. Maybe coming back after R&R has proven too much of an adjustment. Maybe I've been here too long. I have trouble registering any commitment. The only satisfaction I've had in the past few weeks was knocking Major Cattley off the balcony. That had real purpose. Vietnam doesn't.

The IRA had resolve, yet I see the Marine Corps struggle. Why? Because America is indifferent toward its efforts. The press is hostile, and the average American doesn't want to be bothered.

Such concerns never entered my mind when Captain Klein commanded. It was a "pay me, point me, I'll kill anybody you want me to" attitude. We had but one objective: close with and destroy the enemy. But under Captain Parker it is now "pay me, protect me, make me look good." It's amazing how the self-serving leadership style of one man can decimate the spirit of such a good organization.

Somehow I feel lost in a sea of confusion. I think back of the satisfying times in the IRA, and the excitement of coming to America and joining the Marine Corps. I've gained a wealth of experience in the years since I left university. Happy times...yes, full of direction and dedication. But now all of that has disappeared. I serve without resolve, as do the others in the company.

It didn't surprise me when Captain Parker called for me later in the day. This time he had prepared. He briefed me on the mission, adding particulars on current intelligence data—the NVA battalion that punished our company still operated in the vicinity. I question whether our battalion knows of his plan.

This will be my last diary entry until I return. I have much to do before we go through the protective wire at 2400. As I make preparations, I can't help but wonder if Captain Parker might have programmed my demise.

Colonel Jason Davis put down the smudged legal pad. He clinched his fists as an overwhelming sense of anger and sorrow gripped him.

CHAPTER 18

Ned O'Shea straggled back to his platoon after receiving Captain Parker's orders. He felt like it was the year 50 A.D. and someone had just made him a participant in the Roman games at the Coliseum. He saw his odds as about that good.

He called his platoon sergeant and squad leaders together and briefed them on their upcoming mission. When he'd finished, they looked at him with unbelieving eyes. They knew their lieutenant hadn't hatched this ill-favored scheme, but they realized too that he always gave orders as though they were coming from him: to do otherwise would undermine the company's command structure.

"Sir, we have a number of inexperienced men who are pretty spooked. They know the clobbering the NVA already gave the platoon. They might not be too reliable in a pinch," Sergeant Gilmore said.

"I sense that, Sergeant Gilmore," Ned said. "We'll just have to dispel what fears we can and keep them occupied. Maybe a positive attitude on our part will settle them down. In the meantime, we have a lot to do before dark. Make sure the men clean their weapons and draw a double unit of ammo. And have them carry two canteens plus assault rations for two days. If time permits, see if they can grab some shut-eye before we move out." His voice trailed off as his tired and uncertain eyes reflected a hollow gaze.

Those who knew him had never witnessed such a distant and detached air about Ned O'Shea. When the chips were down, the lieutenant had always pulled them through. Somehow, this time it seemed different. He took on the semblance of someone just going through the motions...and it scared them.

Sharply at midnight, the platoon silently moved in column through the company's protective wire.

Prior to their departure, Ned coordinated his movement with the platoon commanders on his right and left flanks. They wished him luck and openly expressed their doubts about his mission. Although he shared them, he gave no response to their comments.

The platoon numbered only 29 men. They carried no crew-served weapons; Captain Parker wanted them mobile and denied them an attached machine gun section and 60mm mortars. And they carried no LAWs, the 66mm light anti-tank weapon, an inferior U.S. equivalent to the North Vietnamese RPG (rocket propelled grenade).

Ned knew he'd be terribly outgunned if he made contact. His only hope was to move stealthily and to avoid a fire fight.

Fifteen-hundred meters north, northwest of Golf Company's position, the terrain rose sharply. Ned wanted to reach the military crest of Hill 597 before daylight. From there he could scan the surrounding country and use the hill as a base from which to send out patrols.

The night was clear and still. As the platoon moved into the shadows, Marines in the company outposts listened to the muffled rustling of the men's combat gear. Soon the sounds drifted away as the darkness absorbed the 29 men as though it was a giant sponge. One moment they were there; the next they were gone.

Ned intended to follow a woodcutter's trail to the hill to avoid crashing through the jungle at night and alerting the enemy. He knew the NVA could have mined the trail, but it was a chance he had to take.

Ned feared mines the most. It seemed the enemy placed them everywhere, giving little concern as to who might trip them. Often Ned saw the mangled bodies of young children and their mothers. He'd lost 47 men in the past 15 months, over half of them to mines. They'd left Vietnam in body bags or stretchers, their maimed and bloodied figures stoic and gray with the pallor of death. Most often, they were missing body parts—arms, legs, eyes, testicles. War is a dirty business. Ruthless, uncaring and unselective, it takes young and old, smart and dumb. And it requires indifference from those who wage it. To dwell on the cause and effect of their actions would overwhelm any sane man's ethos.

The multitude of stars threw an eerie light on the silent, snaking column of Marines as they moved slowly toward their initial objective. Hour after hour, the symphony of muted moves rhythmically emitted the same sounds. Periodically, the column would halt and the men would, as if on queue, immediately take cover on either side of the trail. Most had no idea why they'd stopped; they only feared that somehow danger had engulfed them. Then, as quickly as they'd moved off the trail, they were up again and moving.

Finally, their sharp ascent told them they were climbing the southeast side of Hill 597. Hunched over, they plodded slowly and silently up its face.

The platoon wound its way to a point 75 meters from the hill's summit. There, the jungle canopy gradually broke open, exposing a cratered terrain of splintered trees, water filled shell holes and oozing red clay.

Incipient traces of light signaled the beginning of nautical morning twilight. Soon the sun would rise and erase the cover of darkness that had shielded them.

Ned motioned his squad leaders up and directed them to deploy their men around the summit, keeping 50% of them alert and allowing the others to sleep.

He then took Sergeant Gilmore, a fire team from the 1st squad and his radio operator to the hill's crest and waited for enough light to survey the terrain below him. He hoped to see some sign of enemy movement, some tell-tale clue of the elusive NVA battalion.

Resting his back against a shattered stump, Ned pulled his knees against his chest and steadied his binoculars against his eyes. He rotated the lenses to the eastern sky and fixed them on the planet Venus. She was brightest in the early morning sky. No artificial light diminished his gaze as the amateur astronomer marveled at the heavens...something he'd often done before when checking his platoon's defensive positions at night.

As the light increased, he slowly checked the steaming landscape below him. He first turned his gaze southeast, back toward Golf Company's position. He'd hoped his platoon had moved undetected to the hill, and that the NVA had not sealed off their escape route.

He could see no movement in those open areas between his current position and Captain Parker's. Neither did he see smoke drifting above the jungle canopy. Maybe Lady Luck was with him. "So far so good," he whispered to himself.

He lowered his field glasses and looked over at Sergeant Gilmore. The NCO had fallen asleep against a downed tree. He, like so many veterans, slept whenever the chance presented itself. He appeared exhausted, but Ned knew he was resilient and would be up and moving at the first crack of battle. Even the spoon popping off a grenade was enough to wake any seasoned Marine. It was like a mother conditioned to hearing her baby cry at night. A sixth sense kept them alert, even when asleep.

Moving his body around the stump, Ned steadied his binoculars on a region south and west of the hill. Slowly and deliberately, he moved the glasses short distances and carefully studied the twisted and tortured landscape—a jaded Venus.

He moved again and began to search to the west and northwest. Methodically scanning each hill and valley, he strained to detect something unusual, some fleeting evidence of the enemy's disposition.

Nothing.

Ned felt exhaustion creeping into his limbs, and his head began to nod. Startled by his sudden fatigue, he looked around at his small contingent. Sergeant Gilmore hadn't moved. The radio operator likewise was out. The fire team slept too, except for one rifleman, a new man who'd joined the platoon the day before. Ned didn't even know his name, but their eyes met and a smile of approval crossed Ned's camouflaged face.

The young Marine felt acceptance and smiled back.

CHAPTER 19

While Ned O'Shea and his men spent the night on the move, Captain Parker slept soundly in his bunker.

He awoke to the ring of his field telephone located on his fold-out desk. His executive officer quickly answered it and then handed it to the annoyed captain. He told him it was the battalion commander.

Taking the phone from Lieutenant Stewart, the opportunistic and toady officer spoke with an air of patronizing propriety: "Captain Parker here, sir. Can I be of assistance?"

Lieutenant Colonel Flaherty didn't like Parker. He saw through him from day one, and everything he did reinforced his suspicions of Parker's competence and motives.

"I want you at the battalion command post in 30 minutes. In the meantime, give your company a warning order to be ready to move within two hours."

The phone went dead. Parker felt daunted.

He commenced to flail around in the cramped bunker as he tried to dress and at the same time give directions, none of which properly addressed the company's movement.

Lieutenant Stewart kept saying, "Yes, sir" to every absurd utterance from his Boy Scout level leader.

Captain Parker was more concerned with his appearance at the upcoming meeting than anything else.

He shaved with a battery operated razor his wife had given him and put on his last starched utility uniform. He then gazed approvingly at his handsome appearance in a small mirror and combed his wavy hair so that not one strand was out of place.

He confidently strapped on his shoulder holster and turned to his executive officer and rhetorically asked, "How do I look?"

"Splendid, sir," came the predictable response.

Without acknowledging the executive officer's presence, Captain Parker left the bunker and marched rigidly to the battalion command post, timing his entrance so as to be the last company commander to appear. He wanted all to notice him, as though it was a signal for the battalion commander to begin since the anointed one had arrived.

No one paid any attention to him. They were sullen and preoccupied with the upcoming mission. The other three rifle company commanders were seasoned veterans. Aged beyond their years, they uniformly appeared gaunt and wearied, but each had fierceness about him. It spelled the mission oriented mentality they needed to survive as both a company and a battalion. Captain Parker didn't fit.

The cragginess of the battalion commander's tone reflected the criticality of his message.

"Gentlemen, we're pulling out of our present positions at 0800. HMM 262 will transport us to the demilitarized zone in the vicinity of Route 1. Appears Charlie is moving substantial forces into the region for a possible major push south. We'll set up blocking positions to thwart his efforts. It's critical that we're in position ASAP to stop any drive. Hopefully, we'll have reinforcements in a day or so. Right now, the Vietnamese Marine Corps has remnants of a battalion in the immediate vicinity. We can't expect too much help because they're pretty well shot up.

"The S-3 will brief you on the details of our deployment. The S-4 has the sequence of the lift. We'll start with Echo Company, followed by Golf and Foxtrot. Hotel will cover our departure and will leave last. Any questions?"

A myriad of queries went through everyone's mind, but they knew it was not the time for casual discussions, so all remained silent...their eyes fixed forward.

That was the formal side of the house. The informal side of the communications coin had another scenario.

Rumors fly and the scuttlebutt within the rank and file had it that the battalion was moving.

Small groups of men began to discuss the prospect. Anticipation reigned, and they all speculated about where they were heading.

The discussions had a more somber tone within Golf Company. Lance Corporal Browning and several other lower ranking enlisted men felt apprehensive. They knew

Lieutenant Kagan's platoon was somewhere to their west. Were they abandoned, sent on a suicide mission or what?

They worried about this mainstay of the company and how his uncommon leadership contrasted with the new guy in command. They missed their old skipper, Captain Klein. Several mused about the stupid mission he'd sent the third platoon on, and how insecure they felt with Captain Parker at the helm.

The men's morale was down, way down.

Regretfully, at such times, unit cohesion begins to unravel, and it had reached that point in Golf Company.

Private Jimmy Holden, a slow-talking North Carolinian was the first to sally an opinion.

"This company has really gotten fucked up since Captain Parker took over. The men in my squad refer to him as 'Captain Richard Cranium' and think the fucker is either nuts or out to get us all killed."

"Things have sure changed since Captain Klein, and the other officers got killed," said Lance Corporal Jack Christensen. "I really miss the way things used to run. Now I'm not sure what's going on. I really want out of this outfit."

"Is there anything we can do at our level?" asked a new private who had joined the company that day.

"Frag his ass!" blurted Private Richard Jones. "Someone should roll a grenade under fucking Richard Cranium's cot and blow his ass away. That way we wouldn't have to put up with all this confusion shit."

Jones had a court-martial on his record and four non-judicial punishments. He was a Project 100,000 draftee and a borderline idiot. He had a simple and violent solution to any problem.

Things hadn't gotten that bad and the other men dismissed his suggestion without further comment. They put Jones in the same category as Captain Parker: dangerous. Other suggestions arose. Might they defecate in Captain Parker's mess kit or pour gasoline into his canteen? The solutions were all banal, immature and unimaginative.

The conversation ended, and the parties drifted back to their respective squads without having decided who would do what, if anything.

It was all idle talk, and no one gave the discussion another thought except for Lance Corporal Browning. He felt great loyalty and admiration for Lieutenant Kagan, and resolved to even the score with Captain Parker.

Meanwhile, the operations and logistics officers collectively briefed all hands on the specifics of the upcoming mission. The commanders took notes, synchronized their watches and quickly returned to their companies. No one talked with Lester Parker as he watched everyone leave. He felt confused and alone. This was the only assignment he'd had where people didn't render some favoritism toward him. He hadn't realized that he was yet to prove himself. His aristocratic assignments impressed no one in the trenches, and most looked upon him with suspicion.

As he started for his company area, Lieutenant Colonel Flaherty happened to intersect Parker's route. The battalion commander didn't mince words. A direct, no-nonsense officer, he quickly synthesized information garnered from years of experience in two wars. He had to know how to deploy each unit, depending on its personality. Captain Klein was one type of leader, but with Parker, he had reservations.

"Les, I haven't time for much talk, nor do you, but I want a quick assessment of your company. You've had a few days to survey your outfit. How would you rate them? Can they do the job?" asked the battalion commander, his pale, marble blue eyes staring through those of his new company commander. He directed his question at Parker's abilities as much as he did that of Golf Company's.

"Sir, I have all new leaders, except for one platoon commander. Three of my officers are boot second lieutenants, and they lack experience. My executive officer and first sergeant are the best. The company has had a major turnover in the last month," Parker replied, all the while maintaining a haughty air.

The colonel looked at him in anticipation, awaiting more information, but Parker offered none.

"You haven't answered my question, captain."

"Sir, I believe I have," Parker responded, still holding his baronial poise.

"I wanted to know how you rate them and if they can do the job. You didn't answer the mail except to provide me some peripheral bullshit," Flaherty barked.

"They are inexperienced but can do the job, sir," came Parker's reply.

"Do you have any problems, captain?" the colonel continued.

"Just one sir. It's Lieutenant Kagan. He's salty—a troublemaker who has tried to turn the other officers against me," Parker answered. The moment he said it, he realized he'd slipped.

"You'd better go back to the drawing board, captain. Kagan is the best platoon commander in this battalion. He's smart, tough, vicious and loyal." The colonel put emphasis on "loyal" and continued. "You haven't read him right, and you'd be well-advised to use him as an asset rather than thinking he's causing unrest. Know your men, captain; that's elementary for any competent leader. Regretfully, you don't know Lieutenant Kagan," the colonel concluded in obvious disgust.

Before Parker could amplify his statement, the colonel walked away from him.

Stunned by his inept exchange with his battalion commander, Lester Parker walked back to his bunker with a lifeless expression on his flushed face.

His appearance alarmed Lieutenant Stewart, who in turn registered concern for his commander.

"Is everything all right, sir?"

Captain Parker emitted an unintelligible grunt and then sat on his cot staring at the bulkhead immediately in front of him.

So unnerved was Charles Stewart that he simply left the bunker.

Meanwhile, Lester Parker realized someone else had his number. He knew he was vain and self-serving, but up to now, he had masked this facade by his patronizing and professional rapport. He felt like a charlatan—probably because he was.

His instinct was to strike back like he did with Lieutenant Kagan. Somehow he wanted to make Lieutenant Colonel Flaherty look bad to counteract any negative impressions he might convey to superiors about him. He thought of dropping subtle hints to key staff members at division headquarters as to Flaherty's fatigue and his inability to continue in command. Maybe he could even talk to his old boss, the division commander. He didn't want to approach the regimental commander because he understood that he and Flaherty were tight.

While he sat brooding, the rest of the battalion was hurriedly preparing for its departure to the DMZ. With great alacrity and precision, they formed into helo-teams and moved to designated assembly areas to await the CH-46 medium helicopters.

The members of Golf Company began to show concern when they saw the companies on either flank pull out of their positions and move to the rear and out of sight.

The stupid first sergeant even began to wonder what might be underway.

"Lieutenant Stewart, what's happening?" he bellowed.

"I don't know First Sergeant Gunther. I'm sure the skipper will brief us in due time."

After 45 minutes, Lieutenant Stewart returned to Captain Parker's bunker. One of the new platoon commanders had talked with a lieutenant in Echo Company who told him the battalion was moving out. Stewart figured he better find out if Golf Company was going too.

He mustered up his strength and walked into the bunker. He found Parker in the same posture, eyes fixed dead ahead.

"Sir, the battalion seems to be on the move, and I was wondering if we're going with them," he said in an inquisitive voice.

Captain Parker looked up at him and blinked. When he suddenly realized his procrastination and lack of priorities had left Golf Company behind the power curve, he acted.

Quickly standing up and wringing his hands, he told his executive officer to call the other officers to the bunker at once. Wild-eyed, Captain Parker set into motion a comical and uncoordinated effort to move his company north.

Lester Parker briefed his lieutenants in disjointed phrases that left them confused as to what exactly he wanted. They began to ask questions which only caused him to fly into a rage. Unsure and dispirited, the three officers went back to their platoons and attempted to bring some order to the directions they'd received.

Charles Stewart felt deeply troubled as the other officers filed out. He stood looking at Captain Parker, perplexed by his superior's volatile and bizarre behavior.

Stewart had concluded that Parker was truly an inept and evil person—unethical and self-serving. He felt revulsion both by the man and by the way he had personally kowtowed to him.

Never before had he questioned Captain Parker, either at division headquarters or since they had joined Golf Company. But he was compelled to do so now.

"Captain Parker, sir: I know you're busy, but what about Lieutenant Kagan and his platoon?"

Parker wheeled about. His executive officer could tell by his expression that he hadn't even thought of Kagan's absence from the company.

"Sir, don't you think we should advise battalion we're short one platoon?"

Parker's puzzled expression turned to hatred. He could not tolerate any subordinate questioning him. He saw such persons as only threats: ones he had to either destroy or subjugate. And he did so in the coarsest possible manner.

"Listen, you fucking pimp. When I need guidance from you, I'll ask for it! In the interim, keep your fucking mouth shut and prepare the company headquarters section for departure. Do you understand?

"And one more thing...if you ever speak to anyone about the third platoon, I'll write you a fitness report that will finish you!"

Lieutenant Stewart immediately reverted to his lap-dog caricature. He would not jeopardize his career, even if, by so doing, it put Kagan and his men at risk.

At 0800, the helicopter squadron's birds began to arrive and Echo Company started to board the aircraft. Golf Company was next, but they hadn't reached their designated assembly area.

The battalion commander watched Echo Company depart and then asked the S-3 the whereabouts of Golf Company. The operations officer could only say they hadn't arrived yet. Enraged, Lieutenant Colonel Flaherty called Captain Parker on the battalion's tactical radio net but could get no answer.

The battalion operated with precision. Knowledge, hard work and exactness made it that way. And if ever its timing faltered, Flaherty was on the problem immediately and corrected it.

He knew something was askew and started for Golf Company's position. Before he had gone 10 meters, an aberration hit the skyline 200 meters to his front.

Golf Company emerged like a contingent of hippies at Woodstock: disorganized, leaderless and everybody doing his own thing. There was no formation or any type of order. One couldn't distinguish platoons or helo-teams or who was in charge. They just converged on the landing zone.

Lieutenant Colonel Flaherty watched as the absurd element lurched toward the awaiting aircraft and boarded. It had an air of uncertainty about it. The men looked tentative and confused, like they didn't know what they were doing. He marveled at their change in discipline and organization since Captain Klein's death.

By late afternoon, the battalion reached its new positions along the DMZ, north of the village of Nam Dong. As Lieutenant Colonel Flaherty conferred with his staff to assess the battalion's needs for the next 48 hours, his sergeant major made ready a case of non-judicial punishment referred to the battalion by Golf Company.

When the battalion commander finally took time about 1900 to eat some cold combat rations, Sergeant Major Steiner approached him.

"Sir, can you hold an Article 15 on a man from Golf Company?" came a sheepish query.

"Sergeant Major, I know when you're dead serious and when you're not. This must be something bizarre. What's the charge?"

"Disrespect toward a superior officer, sir. Captain Parker recommends trial by Special Court-Martial," said the sergeant major.

"What did the man do?"

"Sir, he dicked Captain Parker's canteen cup."

"He what!"

"Sir, the company executive officer saw the captain's radio operator remove the skipper's canteen cup from its pouch and then rub his penis around its rim."

"God help me," murmured the exasperated colonel. "We'll hold office hours at 2200 in my tent."

Lieutenant Colonel Flaherty knew this act indicated a deep morale problem with at least one Marine or even within the company as a whole. Would something worse follow? He feared he was seeing the incipient indicators of a company disintegrating. Men will follow a leader in combat so long as they believe in him. He sensed Captain Parker had quickly lost his men's confidence.

Promptly at 2200, Captain Parker, First Lieutenant Stewart, First Sergeant Gunther and Lance Corporal Browning waited 20 meters in front of the colonel's tent. Sergeant Major Steiner approached Captain Parker and told him the colonel wanted to see him.

Parker entered the tent and saw the tired commander sitting behind his field desk. A large candle flickered in the heavy night air and created a hostile vision of the officer behind the desk. Captain Parker felt he was in a dream world until a mosquito buzzed his ear. He slapped at the insect and waited for the colonel to speak.

"Captain Parker, can you give me any particulars about this charge, other than what's on the written report?"

"No sir, it's all there. I want to nip this kind of juvenile behavior in the bud. I want to make an example of this man. I want the men to know I carry the hammer!"

The battalion commander looked at the bug-eyed eccentric in front of him who was steadily convincing him that he was unfit for command.

"Tell the sergeant major to bring in the accused."

Lance Corporal Browning reported to the battalion commander in the dim light of the tent. The confined spaces reeked of body odor, which only added to the strained atmosphere.

Quickly, the battalion commander warned the Marine of his rights under Article 31 of the Uniform Code of Military Justice, and then asked how he pleaded to the alleged charge.

"Guilty, sir!" came Browning's reply.

Captain Parker expected the colonel to immediately refer it to trial as he'd recommended, but the battalion commander didn't.

"Why did you do this, Browning?" asked Lieutenant Colonel Flaherty.

"Sir, it was the only way I could get even with Captain Parker for what he did."

"What was it that made you want to get even with Captain Parker?" asked the battalion commander, his face taking on an inquisitive look.

Captain Parker had not anticipated the colonel questioning Browning. He began to shuffle back and forth and lick his lips, fearing what might occur next.

After a moderate pause, Lance Corporal Browning spoke. "Sir, Captain Parker left the third platoon stranded three thousand meters in front of our old position. They're doomed. We all feel the same thing might happen to the rest of us, sir."

The battalion commander's face reddened and Captain Parker's turned ashen.

"I want everyone to leave except Captain Parker," said Flaherty.

They quickly departed away from the tent and left the two officers very much alone.

"Is there any truth in Browning's words, Captain Parker?"

"Well sir, we'd been highly active in our area of operation and..."

"Cut the bullshit, Captain Parker! Answer my question. Did you leave a platoon behind? And that's Lieutenant Kagan's platoon isn't it?"

The shaken captain emitted a timid, "Yes, sir."

"And what did you intend to do, just leave them to fend for themselves?

"Why wasn't I told?"

"Sir, Lieutenant Kagan is resilient. I figured he would find us in due time," Parker said, as a silly grin and impish laugh followed his inane statement.

"I can't believe it! You mean to tell me you left a whole platoon somewhere out in the bush and expect them to just show up one day?

"I want the coordinates of their location so we can send choppers to extract them at the earliest."

"I don't have them, sir. I haven't had radio contact with the platoon since they departed. They were on a clandestine mission to locate the NVA battalion that mauled the company recently. Only when they spotted Charlie were they to establish radio contact. I can only give you the area of operations I directed Lieutenant Kagan to operate in."

"Captain Parker, I want you to return to your company. I will put the wheels in motion to try and locate Lieutenant Kagan and pull him and his men out of God knows where. In the interim, you'd best be thinking about this whole mess because I intend to relieve you of command once I get this fiasco sorted out.

You've got to be the most inept company commander I have ever known. Your pompous ass isn't worth the powder to blow it apart. Be assured, if one of those men dies, I will personally prefer charges against you and recommend your court-martial. Get out of my sight before I lose it!"

The humiliated officer left the battalion commander's tent and stumbled back to his command post, all the while determined to beat Lieutenant Colonel Flaherty to the punch. He intended to get word to the division commander that his boss had threatened him, and that he was unfit for command because of combat fatigue. This would make the general suspect that Flaherty was no longer capable of rational decisions. Such a perception would nullify any actions the colonel might try after sorting out the Kagan issue.

CHAPTER 20

Ned continued his search of the terrain around Hill 597, but saw nothing unusual. At that moment, another wave of fatigue overcame him, like the wall a marathon runner hits at the 20 mile mark. He couldn't ignore it. He nudged Sergeant Gilmore, told him to take the binoculars and continue scanning the surrounding country while he grabbed some shut-eye.

Immediately, Ned fell into a deep sleep as his platoon sergeant began working the terrain due north, shooting 10 degree azimuths in a clockwise fashion. He searched for some enemy indicators but saw none.

Finally, Sergeant Gilmore reached 150 degrees and found himself looking back at the battalion's trenches. Although the distance was considerable, he could make out some activity. He became alarmed as he watched a large number of CH-46 helicopters descend upon the battalion's position and then exit to the north. He waited for awhile and then saw the choppers return, land, and lift-off again. Part or all of the battalion was leaving.

"Lieutenant Kagan, I hate to wake you, sir, but I think you'd better have a look. Something's going on back at battalion. I've watched two waves of helicopters apparently lift out troops. They're going north," Gilmore said, his voice full of concern.

"Let's see the glasses," O'Shea said, now fully awake.

He looked back at the battalion's position and readily saw what his platoon sergeant noted. He, too, became concerned. The apparent abrupt departure of large numbers of troops indicated an unknown crisis to which the battalion had to respond. The number of helicopter waves also told him that most probably the entire battalion was on the move.

He knew Captain Parker didn't want him on the company radio net until he'd identified enemy movement; regardless, he told the radio operator to raise the company.

The Marine immediately keyed the handset and spoke into the receiver: "Cedar Bird Six, This Is Cedar Bird Three... Over."

No answer.

He tried again, and then again, but he could only hear the handset's numbing hiss in his ear. Either the company didn't have the radio on, or it wasn't monitoring the net. Then again, they could be out of range.

"Sir, no one answers."

Anticipating the platoon commander's questions, he added, "I've reset the frequency and checked the battery. It's not the radio, sir."

Ned O'Shea stood perplexed. The whole time he'd been in Vietnam, he'd never experienced anything like this. But then again, he'd never had a company commander like Captain Parker. The man was so political in nature that he was always anticipating what "his" next move should be, not the company's. Ned felt deep down that Captain Parker had abandoned his platoon. He just hoped Lieutenant Colonel Flaherty would correct things before they got too far out of hand. In the meantime, he needed some answers. He had to determine if the entire battalion left or if Golf Company had remained behind.

He turned to his platoon sergeant. "Sergeant Gilmore, I want you to take a fire team and double back to the battalion area. See if you can find out what's happening. If someone is there with a radio, come up on the net and let me know the status. If the positions are abandoned, pop a red smoke grenade and wait there. We'll join you ASAP. Good luck."

The sergeant, a veteran in his own right, let out a muffled groan, adding "I don't like the smell of this one, Mister Kagan. Charlie is all over the area and we're behind the eight ball if the battalion's gone. I hope they haven't hung us out to dry."

Ned sensed the anxiousness in his platoon sergeant's voice and caught the strained expression on his face.

"Let's not borrow trouble, Sergeant Gilmore. We'll survive."

He didn't believe that anymore than Gilmore did.

Sergeant Gilmore took the fire team that had accompanied them to the summit. They quickly moved down Hill 597 and disappeared into the dense vegetation.

A sick and desperate feeling comes over all combat veterans when they are about to experience battle. The element of the unknown, the mortal danger, the anticipated pain and the separation from loved ones, the thoughts of maimed and lost comrades—they all combine to create a dread that centers in the pit of the stomach. It's an emotion like none other.

Ned O'Shea and Sergeant Gilmore both felt the sensation, but knew how to handle it, namely by throwing themselves into the tasks at hand. The platoon, on the other hand, could only sense their leaders' apprehension and wait with anticipation.

Soon the final helicopters departed and silence overtook the region. Ned could not comprehend why they'd left without his platoon or at least Captain Parker giving him some guidance.

As he wondered, he lifted the binoculars once again and began to search the terrain.

He wasn't the only one scanning the countryside. Major Gia Long Au, commanding officer of the 2d Battalion, 304th NVA Regiment smiled as he too saw the last of the helicopters leave the Marine positions.

He realized the Americans didn't have enough manpower to counter the buildup along the DMZ and also protect the regions west of Route 1. Their departure allowed for a thrust east to the sea, severing their main overland supply artery north from Hue to Quang Tri. Even if his regiment held the region for only a short time, they would inflict a psychological blow on the Americans.

As a member of the Vietminh, forerunner to the North Vietnamese Army, his units did the same thing with the French in the early 1950s. They would isolate French outposts, and then systematically annihilate them. The French reacted like a crazed animal, wildly recoiling, but never isolating or destroying their tormentor.

Major Au's family had spent its whole adult life fighting foreigners. His father and elder brother died at the hands of the Japanese in World War II. He subsequently fought the French and now engaged the Americans. He'd been severely wounded at the battle of Dienbienphu in 1954, shortly before the French surrendered. While recuperating in a hospital for an extended period, he'd read every piece of military literature he could acquire, and steeped himself in the nationalistic aims of Ho Chi Minh. He felt the Vietnamese cause was more than justified. Cunning and fearless, he was determined to see Vietnam as one nation.

He was 41 and small in stature. His dark, sunken eyes and parasitic-ridden body made him look much older. Yet this angular and Lilliputian image masked an unceasing inner drive, intent on defeating the Americans, no matter what it took. Both ruthless and undaunted, he readily sacrificed subordinates to ensure his battalion's success. His men feared and mistrusted him because they knew he regarded them as expendable.

Major Au had a reputation for both high casualties and high successes, going as far back as the days when he led a platoon against the French. Proportionately, he'd lost more men than any other commanding officer in the North Vietnamese Army.

A man of simple pleasures, he had no family except for his aging mother. He seldom saw her, as the army kept him committed to regions well away from her home in the town of Langson, near the Chinese border. She would die in 1979 when the Chinese invaded Vietnam to "teach it a lesson."

Major Au had a profound weakness, which he neither recognized nor accepted, even when counseled: He could not delegate authority. Subordinate unit commanders had to contend with his ubiquitous presence, wherein he would continually countermand their orders and direct their men to perform tasks without their knowledge. His overbearing control destroyed initiative and left his officers confused. This act might have worked at the platoon level and to a limited degree at the company level, but in a battalion it had everyone going in opposite directions at the same time. Yet the battalion had a successful reputation, even though some of the more astute officers suspected it was a matter of time before their luck ran out. Like Golf Company under Captain Parker, Major Au's battalion had a penchant to self-destruct.

The 304th's Regimental Commander, Colonel Thu, had briefed Major Au and the other battalion commanders two days earlier about the potential opportunity to sever the Marines' overland supply route. Major Au's battalion had the lead and would probe for weaknesses in an unsuspecting region. When he sighted the Marines leaving their previous positions southeast of Hill 597, he saw the opening he wanted. He would move into their abandoned positions and then strike east, northeast through Co Bi to Quang Bien, and occupy the village there. This would force the Marines to contend with a major NVA unit operating to their rear and disrupting their supply lines.

As Major Au formulated his plans and told his subordinates what they were to do, Sergeant Gilmore and his fire team arrived at the now deserted battalion positions. He quickly surveyed the area and saw that everyone had gone. There was no sign of life—only discarded "C" ration cans, protective wire and other materiels gave the indication that a major unit had been there.

Immediately, he pulled the pin on a red smoke grenade and tossed it to the highest ground around him. Soon the billowing red cloud from the grenade drifted skyward and caught the eye of Ned O'Shea. Ned's heart sank; Captain Parker had left them behind and on their own in hostile territory.

His watch read 1300. If they left within the hour, they would make it back to Sergeant Gilmore's location before dark, provided they ran into no difficulties.

O'Shea called up his squad leaders and directed them to have the men "saddle-up" and be ready to move. He took one last scan of the region below him. He neither saw nor heard any signs of the enemy. Again, he hoped his luck would hold.

"All right men, let's move out."

The column snaked its way down the steep terrain they had climbed the night before. The heat became as oppressive as the anxiety the men felt. Ned had apprised them of what was happening, although he never shared his thoughts of their abandonment or his distrust of Captain Parker.

The platoon moved with deliberate haste, bordering on reckless abandon. They had to reach safety. Assembling at the battalion's old positions, Ned figured he could move east to Route 1. There he could contact some American units and get a fix on the battalion.

CHAPTER 21

Ned O'Shea felt driven, like no other time in country. It was a race against time, because he knew his bantam-size unit would provide easy pickings for the larger NVA units operating in the region. Had they seen the battalion leave too?

He had no mission now except to save his men. Somehow they understood that, and followed him with total loyalty.

Ned found it difficult to control the anxiety gripping him. They were highly vulnerable, and he knew from previous experience that the enemy wasted little time in moving into abandoned positions. Who would make it there first was the question fixed in his mind?

After an hour's march, the platoon reached a small rise in the valley below. Placing his men around the hill's military crest, he moved to its summit and slowly rose to his knees and again surveyed the land around him.

Insects tormented him as he struggled with his binoculars. Placing them to his eyes, he instantly froze. Looking directly south, he saw in another valley, 800 meters below him, a large enemy formation in what looked like an assembly area. They appeared to be making preparations for a major attack.

Steadily investigating the formation's makeup, he spotted a commander of sorts. Unknown to him, it was Colonel Thu, making one last visit to Major Au's battalion before it moved across the line of departure.

"Sniper up," Ned barked in a constrained tone.

A Marine rifleman quickly came along side him. It was Lance Corporal Larry Tucker, a new man battalion had attached to his platoon days earlier from its scout/sniper platoon.

"What did you fire on the range the last time out, Tucker?" Ned asked, "And no bull shit."

Tucker lowered his head and said, "189, sir."

"You mean you went unqualified with the rifle, and they made you a sniper?"

"Sir, when I reported to the battalion S-1 last week, the administrative chief told me he had vacancies in all the rifle companies and the scout/sniper platoon. He then asked me what I wanted to do, and I told him I wanted to be a scout. So here I am."

"Let me borrow your rifle, Tucker," Ned said.

Taking the .30 caliber M-1 Garand rifle, complete with scope, Ned assumed a prone position. Like his rifle in Ireland, he felt comfortable with it in his hands. He rested the forward end of the stock on his pack and peered into the powerful lens. Slowly, he adjusted the scope to 800 meters.

Then he affixed its cross hairs on Colonel Thu as he stood, hands on his hips, speaking to Major Au.

As if on cue, Colonel Thu turned and momentarily faced him.

Instantly Ned put additional pressure on the trigger and felt the high caliber recoil drive into his shoulder as the deadly projectile raced toward its target.

At such a great range, the bullet, never rising above the elevated axis of the bore, lost velocity and plunged toward the unsuspecting officer.

Colonel Thu caught the round in his neck. It tore through the soft tissue around his voice box and shattered the neck vertebrae.

He collapsed in a heap at the feet of Major Au. He died instantly.

Those around the dead officer scurried for cover as Ned sighted the rifle again. He saw an 82mm mortar section go into action, orienting the tubes in his direction. He put the cross hairs on a soldier stripping powder increments from a mortar round and fired again.

The bullet struck the man's pelvis, tearing open his right iliac artery. He spun around, momentarily standing stunned by the wound and then slowly sank backwards to the ground as his uniform trousers filled with blood, and his eyes took on a fish-eyed stare. Mortal shock overwhelmed his body and he died within minutes as his comrades dove for cover, not knowing who would be the next target.

Ned realized his platoon was vastly outnumbered, and the only thing he had going for his men was speed and stealth. As if they knew their platoon commander's thoughts, the men rose as Ned lifted himself from the deck and started double timing toward Sergeant Gilmore and his men at the battalion's old position.

They never stopped. Running the entire way, the platoon clamored up the final hill to where its platoon sergeant and his fire team waited in trepidation. Some men vomited while others just collapsed in abandoned foxholes, gasping for breath between gulps from their nearly empty canteens.

"Am I glad to see you, lieutenant?" Sergeant Gilmore shouted to the exhausted officer.

Ned looked at him, half dazed and near heat exhaustion. He couldn't smile because both men knew the sorry state they had found themselves.

"I heard what sounded like .30 caliber rounds a while back. I figured it had to be you. About the same time we saw an NVA patrol moving toward our position about 500 meters out. When you started shooting they disappeared into the jungle to the west. I'm sure they were doing a reconnaissance before attacking our position. I have no idea what we're facing lieutenant," the fretful sergeant blurted in octaves higher than his normal voice.

"I think there must be an NVA regiment or at least a battalion southwest of us," Ned said, his chest heaving to breathe. "We saw them from the high ground northwest of here. That's where you heard the firing. We dropped a couple of them and took off at high port to make it back here.

"Hopefully, we confused them enough to bide ourselves some time and figure out a course of action. Did you see any movement to your rear? I ask because I worry whether they have surrounded us," noted Ned, now having caught his breath and thinking logically.

"I don't know lieutenant," said Sergeant Gilmore. "They could be everywhere; there is just too much cover all around us. I think we're in some bad shit, sir!"

Meanwhile, Major Au acted. The fact that some sniper had killed Colonel Thu and one of his mortar men generated two realizations: First, he appreciated that he was now in charge, and secondly, he felt a need to respond.

He didn't confer with his company commanders but personally ordered the entire battalion to march toward the old Marine position. He did this even before his reconnaissance element had reported back.

The battalion started to move, convulsively at first, and then more rhythmically. No one except Major Au knew exactly what they were doing.

Major Au led the column, and he headed as directly as he could toward the former Marine stronghold. He knew the battalion had left and that only remnants remained, if in fact they were Americans at all. Some South Vietnamese Army units could have slid in or a Popular Force element might be scrounging the area, looking for discarded building materials or other such things they could take back to their villages. Whoever was there, he intended to destroy them and continue driving east to cut the American supply route as Colonel Thu had directed them. Only now Colonel Thu couldn't restrain him. He felt free and independent, operating in the environment that best suited his personality.

After fifteen minutes on the march, a new company commander, Captain Tung, came alongside Major Au and while straining to keep up with him, asked what they were doing.

Major Au, never missing a stride, removed his pistol from its holster and wheeled about, striking the unsuspecting officer flush on the chin with its butt. He replaced the pistol and continued the torrid pace to the northeast, leaving the semi-conscious officer lying beside the path, blood spewing from his mouth and the deep gash on the edge of his chin. Within time, his company came alongside their commander's crumpled body, lifted him onto a makeshift stretcher, and carried him forward.

The major's actions surprised only the newcomers. Most of the others knew of his tyrannical demeanor and his inability to have anyone question his judgment. He led by fear—a weak substitute for a positive rapport.

About 1,500 meters from the Marine position, Major Au saw his reconnaissance element running toward the column. He ordered the battalion off the trail, and the column slid to the ground. They were stoic—senses not easily overcome as long as Major Au controlled them.

The reconnaissance patrol reported only four men in the former Marine position. Major Au smiled, knowing he had a walk in the sun in front of him. He would overrun the positions occupants and immediately strike east and sever Route 1.

He called Captain Tung to the front. By this time the captain had regained some form of consciousness and a pressure bandage had slowed the bleeding on his chin. He stared at Major Au with hatred as the gaunt commander flashed a sardonic smile and directed him to commence a frontal assault immediately.

Captain Tung knew he could not question the order. He returned to his company, determined to accomplish his mission with the utmost haste and efficiency.

Double timing his men past the battalion, the 100-man company disappeared around a corner in the trail leading to the former Marine position. Five hundred meters from his objective he stopped his men. He would give them a final rest and an opportunity to gather their bearings before they launched their assault.

Major Au offered no supporting arms for the attack. He figured the company RPGs and its machine guns would provide all the covering fire the company needed. Captain Tung took note of this and considered his best chance for success would be to attack with three platoons abreast. By firing and maneuvering, they could sweep over the lightly defended position with ease.

After briefing his officers and allowing ten minutes rest, the company rose to its feet and moved 300 meters to its attack position. This would be the last cover they would have before assaulting Ned's position.

Again, Captain Tung allowed his men to take a short rest and make final preparations before crossing the line of departure, the point where they would come into view of the Marines.

The NVA company would have to cover almost 200 meters before reaching their assault position at the base of the fortified hill. Here they would make their final charge and overrun the four defenders.

Captain Tung's men had not moved without notice. Ned had deployed his men as soon as they had gotten their wind and although unaware of the pending attack, nevertheless were positioned well to cope with any eventuality.

As the North Vietnamese crossed the line of departure, Private Harry Deward, a lanky farm boy from Winterset, Iowa shouted, "Here they come, lieutenant!" His voice alerted the entire platoon and all hands immediately faced to the west. The Marine saw a column of troops fan out into three platoons abreast and break into a slow gate. At that moment, Captain Tung's machine guns opened up, firing from fixed positions on either side of the advancing troops.

"Standby and make every shot count," shouted Ned as bullets split the air above his men.

The Marines waited for their lieutenant to give the order to fire. When the situation presented itself, he made them all feel like they were on a rifle range by the commands he gave.

"Ready on the right! Ready on the left! Already on the firing line! Watch your targets!"

Each man took careful aim, their battle sight set at 300 meters. They would target their enemy a bit low.

At 150 meters from their objective, Captain Tung had his accompanying RPGs fire their first salvo. The rockets arched onto the Marine positions and exploded. Shell fragments laced the perimeter but hit only one Marine, causing a flesh wound on his left shoulder.

It was time to act: Ned O'Shea gave the order to commence firing.

As the entire position erupted in a simultaneous crescendo of rifle fire, Captain Tung watched in terror as 73 of his men went down in the first fusillade. They pitched in all directions or simply dropped in place. The Marines' M-16 rifles' .223 caliber rounds with their 55 grain bullets traveled at tremendous velocity, over 3,200 feet per second and generated almost 1,300 foot pounds of energy. The small size of the bullets made them spin erratically whenever they would hit a target, and the tumbling and ricocheting rounds would cause massive and jagged wounds that were often lethal.

Captain Tung readily realized too late that the objective had far more than four men on it. He also knew that major Au's intelligence report was bad or that maybe the battalion commander had deliberately programmed him to fail.

Whatever, he struggled to extract the remaining men from the killing zone in which they suddenly found themselves.

While his machine guns continued firing and the remaining RPG rounds raced toward the Marine positions, Captain Tung directed a retreat. His men needed no encouragement and the orderly withdrawal turned into a route.

Some men, crazed with fear, rose and ran to the rear only to be cut down by the Marine marksmen. Others began to crawl and eventually reached higher vegetation. It concealed their movements and allowed them to find sanctuary.

Captain Tung joined them shortly, to find that only 13 of his men had made it to safety. All of his officers and senior enlisted men were either dead or lying mortally wounded in front of the Marine lines. The remaining men were shaken and distrustful. They believed the young officer had foolishly led the company to its destruction. He sensed their disgust and wished he'd died in the ill-fated attack.

Meanwhile, Major Au, hearing the heavy volume of fire, started to march the remainder of the battalion toward what he figured was Captain Tung's newly won objective.

He moved confidently forward. As he rounded a curve in the trail, he came face-to-face with an anxious Captain Tung, accompanied by a dozen equally terrified men.

The battalion stopped but Major Au continued on to the disheveled captain.

"Where is the rest of your company, Captain Tung?" barked Major Au.

"They are dead, Major Au, except for the ones with me."

"I'll have you shot!" came the major's response.

Captain Tung's deliberate response showed he felt no fear of Major Au now. Confident that he was an able and loyal soldier, he'd been unjustly assaulted and humiliated by what he considered a raving maniac. He precisely followed Major Au's orders and lost his company because of it. Now he stood defiant and full of hatred for his impulsive commander.

The young captain had tried, as best he could, to do what he was ordered to do. No one could have asked for more…except Major Au.

Again the major exploded. "I'll have you shot!"

"Go right ahead, but what did you expect when you sent me to take a hill defended by only four men, and I find a swarm of Marines on it? You deceived me! You gave me erroneous intelligence and then directed me to assault the position immediately. You led me to believe that accomplishing the task would be a minor annoyance at best.

"I am responsible for what happened, but you are ultimately responsible, Major Au."

The major knew his company commander was right, but he refused to acknowledge he'd done anything wrong. Instead, he directed Captain Tung to report to the regimental rear area and await his further action.

As Major Au considered his next move, Ned O'Shea contemplated his. The third platoon had stopped an NVA company dead in its tracks, but Ned felt confident it was but a forewarning of more ominous events.

He considered striking out to Route 1, east of his present position and making contact with any friendly unit he could find. He discussed this with Sergeant Gilmore and then decided they'd best move at the earliest.

As he was about to give a warning order to his men in preparation for their departure, he heard the faint sound of a Huey approaching his position. The familiar chopping sound grew louder and the image of the helicopter magnified as it drew closer.

The sun was starting to fade behind the mountains to the west, and Ned knew they had only two hours of daylight left at the most. He continued to feel uneasy, but hoped the chopper's visit would bring relief or direction of some sort.

Soon the greenish bird settled in the old battalion landing zone and the battalion's assistant operations officer jumped out. It was Captain Ed Sloan, a new officer in the unit. Ned ran over to him and ended up on the receiving end of a rapid message emitted by the skittish captain. Captain Sloan's instructions were to see if the third platoon had returned to the battalion's former position and if so, to instruct Ned to hold until morning. At that time the Air Liaison Officer could dispatch enough uncommitted helicopters to extract them.

As the two officers spoke, one of Ned's fire teams raced to the helicopter and off loaded weapons, ammunition, combat rations and five gallon water cans.

It was obvious Captain Sloan wanted to leave as soon as possible, but Ned stared at him fiercely and said nothing.

The unproven officer read the message in the determined lieutenant's eyes and waited for him to speak.

"Captain Sloan, I don't know if we can hold until morning. Shortly before you arrived, we beat back an NVA company-sized attack. There are plenty more where they came from. The men are exhausted. We need help now. Do you understand? We need it now!"

Pausing for a moment and realizing he had to be more than just a courier, Captain Sloan looked down and pawed the earth with his right foot. He then shot a quick glance back at Ned. "I understand lieutenant. I will relate the severity of your situation to the battalion commander and have relief on the way tonight, if that's possible."

"Thank you, sir," came Ned's abbreviated reply. Even though terse, Captain Sloan sensed the sincerity in Ned's voice and smiled at him. Knowing the captain was his only hope at this juncture, Ned came to attention and executed a genuine salute which the captain returned. He readily realized how much the young officer and his men depended upon him for their very existence.

As Captain Sloan boarded the helicopter, Ned darted back to his platoon's command post, about 50 meters from the landing zone. He turned to watch the Huey lift off and muttered under his breath that he hoped the captain could pull some weight with the battalion S-3 and Lieutenant Colonel Flaherty.

Regretfully, Major Au had not remained passive after learning of Captain Tung's debacle. He too saw the helicopter land at Ned's position and had his 82mm mortar platoon prepare to fire on the hill.

As untimely and disastrous as Captain Tung's attack on Ned's platoon proved, Major Au's decision to mortar the position was just as opportune. The initial rounds fell in the vicinity of the landing zone, and just as the Huey lifted off and turned three feet off the deck to head north, a round hit close to the bird's nose. It killed the pilot, and before the wounded copilot could take control, a second NVA round hit square on the rotor.

The helicopter crashed and exploded, spewing parts across the perimeter. The remaining men aboard died on impact.

As Ned and his men dove for cover, he realized their hope for relief that night had vanished with the flaming remnants of the helicopter. A sense of despair overpowered him, even in this time of terror.

The mortar attack continued sporadically for thirty minutes. Then Ned heard a sickening cry. "Charlie's on the eastern side of the perimeter," came a shout from Corporal Sidney Clark, leader of the platoon's third squad.

Major Au had deployed his battalion so that Ned and his men were surrounded. They were in a noose, and Ned recognized the familiar tactic. Whenever the NVA recognized they were up against a weaker organization they would move rapidly and annihilate it before help could arrive. He's seen the results on Popular Force and ARVN units in the past. He lamented that he hadn't taken his men to the east before the helicopter arrived. The hesitation cost them the advantage. His mind raced; what could they do?

CHAPTER 22

Two hours after Captain Sloan left on his ill-fated flight, Captain Parker took a high-risk gamble. Contrary to his battalion commander's orders, he surreptitiously boarded an administrative flight bound for Da Nang. He planned to pay an unannounced visit on his old boss, the division commander.

Lieutenant Colonel Flaherty knew Parker was inept, but he failed to detect the degree of his disloyalty and ruthlessness. The colonel was to used to officers, good and bad, conforming to the system.

But Captain Parker didn't operate by the system. He was ambitious and above it and subtlety manipulated it to his advantage. Thus far, it had worked; however, he knew this act of desperation put him in the big leagues. It provided him his only chance to save both his command and his career, even if it meant unjustly bringing down his battalion commander.

Bounding off the helicopter after it touched down at the division's landing pad, the determined officer darted toward the division commander's quarters, located nearby the command center.

Major General Thomas Walker sat at a small field desk in his tent going over detailed intelligence reports his G-2 had recently given him. Aged and methodical, the general had a jaded look about him; however, it masked a brilliant and cunning mind, one which kept everyone on their toes. Erudite and astute, he'd synthesized incredible amounts of information from years of experience and made keen and logical decisions about both personnel and operational matters...and he did not suffer fools kindly.

Lester Parker went right to general's hatch and called, "General Walker, it's Captain Lester Parker, and I need to speak with you immediately on a matter of the utmost importance."

Startled, the division commander wasn't used to such interruptions by outsiders, which he considered Captain Parker at this juncture. Although no longer his aide, the two had developed a composed rapport; the general made it a point not to become close to any subordinate. A veteran of the Pacific campaigns of World War II and Korea, he'd seen about everything and had little time for anything outside genuine Marine business.

"Sit down Captain Parker," came an aloof reply to the captain's plea.

"Before you say anything, let me ask if you've gone through your battalion and regimental commanders before coming here?"

The general was not about to entertain someone jumping the chain-of-command. Such actions only undermine the command structure and ultimately destroy unit cohesion.

"General, this is a life and death situation. My battalion commander, Lieutenant Colonel Flaherty has lost it, and I honestly believe he is unfit to command any longer. He....."

"Wait just a minute Captain Parker. You're making serious allegations about a superior behind his back. Have you talked with him about whatever it is that brought you here?"

"Yes I have General Walker, but he was totally out of touch. He is either crazy or trying to destroy me because he knows I'm way ahead of him on all tactical and administrative matters. He directed me to send a platoon on a combat reconnaissance patrol and then pulled the battalion out, leaving them stranded. Now he's trying to blame me for their possible demise.

"Either he's been in the bush too long or resents my political connections."

General Walker sat and looked at his former aide in disbelief. He personally knew Parker's battalion commander and of course his regimental commander. Both were seasoned and battle-hardened officers with superior judgment. Now this dandy fellow had tried to cast a different light on the 1st Marine Regiment's command structure.

He figured Lester had screwed-up big time but remained reticent to tell him so. He didn't want to jeopardize the actions he or subordinate commanders would take in the case;

however, he knew, by the captain's actions, that he'd do anything to save his hide, to include going over his head too by contacting his Washington relatives. Unemotionally and precisely, he wanted to be able to explain his command's actions and have no one question them.

Without saying anything, the division commander rang his EE-8 field telephone and told the switchboard operator to patch him through to the assistant division commander, Brigadier General Thomas Ludwig.

"Tom, I want you to come to my quarters right away," was all General Walker said.

He then sent Captain Parker back to his battalion and, in an indifferent manner, advised him he'd look into his complaint.

Lester Parker was too naive and myopic to realize he'd simply provided the general the wherewithal to seal his fate. As he walked from the tent, he had a childish bounce in his step and a coy smile on his thin lips. Lacking the ability to comprehend that the system had no tolerance for his kind, he went off into the darkness as though he'd dodged a bullet and sensed that some degree of normalcy would return to his strained existence. He somehow envisioned himself a hero, overcoming the actions of uncouth and incompetent commanders.

Shortly after Captain Parker departed, the assistant division commander reported to General Walker.

Brigadier General Thomas Ludwig was a highly cultured and reserved officer who took a measured approach to all his undertakings. He could not hide his feelings, even though he might say nothing. His eyes were his giveaway. They seemed to change color with his mood and at times took on a dark and foreboding air when he became incensed.

"Tom, my former aide, Lester Parker, just paid me an unannounced visit. He claims Lieutenant Colonel Flaherty up in the Second Battalion, First Marines has lost it and is no longer competent to command.

"I want you to leave at the earliest and check into the First Marines. Tell me if they have it in one bag, particularly the Second Battalion.

"Tom, I know you'll give me an objective assessment. Play it low-keyed. I want this basically between you and myself.

"I must give you my impressions of this situation. I inherited Lester Parker; it was 'suggested' that he become my aide before he ever arrived in country, and then I was to ensure he got a rifle company the last half of his tour. I think he has gotten himself into a world of shit up there and is trying to pull strings to save his ass. You're probably asking yourself why I didn't just throw his fanny out of my tent and put him on report. It isn't that simple. He's connected Tom, well connected and while the system must remain true, we cannot be slipshod in doing what we have to do. His professional demise could generate a full blown congressional inquiry. And what the Marine Corps doesn't need at this juncture in the war is to end up embarrassed by some impulsive decision generated by poor judgment.

"Do you understand from where I'm coming?"

General Ludwig saw things as black and white, and he felt uneasy with the talk of political connections. Although not ignorant of such leverage, he nevertheless became uncomfortable when these influences tainted the structure of the Marine Corps. It sickened him to think of spending valuable time covering the Corps' backside to ensure some inept captain received more attention than he rightfully deserved. Even so, he swallowed hard, came to the position of attention and told General Walker that he understood his assignment and would report back to him at the earliest.

After the assistant division commander left his quarters, General Walker took a bottle of bourbon from his footlocker and poured a hefty glass and stared at its contents. He slowly swirled it around and then bit down on an unlit cigar. The war was tough and it required dedicated and competent officers and men to win it. He thought of recent fragging incidents: the killing of unit leaders by undisciplined troops. Although few in number, it still alarmed him that such rot slipped through boot camp and was now in his division. Thanks to the Secretary of Defense and his Project 100,000, illiterate and untrainable men crept into the ranks and proved a disaster in combat. Too slow to grasp either discipline or the gravity of tactical situations, they became burdens, endangering unit safety, cohesion and morale.

General Walker was very tired. He'd too felt the spark slip from the goal before him. He knew that both he and his Marines were fighting a lonely and convoluted war. The United States experienced no deprivations because of it and therefore paid little attention to the daily trauma. The Jane Fonda types sickened him by their outrageous political conduct, and he wondered seriously how a great nation could divide itself at such a critical phase in its history. The Vietnam cause had honor but honor seemed like a weary virtue anymore.

His eyes moistened as he thought of Army General George Marshall's words, "It is not enough to fight. It is the spirit which we bring to the fight that decides the issue. It is morale that wins the victory." He feared the Corps' élan was waning in Vietnam and he felt powerless to affect it,

He paused and took a large swig from the glass and felt a warming sensation slowly travel the length of his thorax. In the distance he heard a helicopter rise from its landing pad and he wondered if either Tom Ludwig or Lester Parker was on it.

Captain Parker was indeed on it. He had bypassed the division headquarters and instead checked out the 1st Medical Battalion's Collecting and Clearing Company located nearby. Fortunately, a medical evacuation helicopter had just deposited several wounded infantrymen from the 1st Marines' area and was headed back in that direction. As it lifted into the clear night sky, Lester Parker felt secure and confident in his recent actions and just knew that he had become a power in his own right.

Brigadier General Thomas Ludwig laid on a helicopter for first light and decided to spend the remainder of the evening developing the questions and procedures he'd follow when he looked into Lester Parker's allegations. He didn't know the captain, but he respected General Walker's judgment and figured his earthy assessment of his former aide probably painted a very true picture. Even so, he would remain objective and deal only in facts, ensuring the officer would receive a fair hearing.

Following the shoreline bordering the East China Sea, the MedEvac chopper traced the rocky heights and darkened crevices which stood defiant against the shrouded waves tugging at the jagged bond below them.

Lester Parker peered through the hatch on the helicopter's starboard side, ignoring the door gunner, and marveled at the rising moon's reflection off the vast ocean below him. Emotionally charged and confident, his euphoria sent chills over his body. He was not happy commanding a rifle company in combat and knew in his heart that he didn't measure up to his fellow commanders, but they were pedestrian and lacked personal vision. They didn't possess the climbing ambition which drove him and would never have taken the chance he just had. And for that reason, Lester Parker felt superior. It was just a matter of time before all of this was behind him and he could return to the states, wear dress uniforms and hopefully obtain some other high visibility job which would mean accelerated promotions. He knew women would swoon over his appearance and manly demeanor as a combat veteran.

The pilot, looking to the west, saw explosions in the far distance and tracer rounds arching from a small perimeter. He assumed some unit was under attack and was firing its final protective fires. Had Lester Parker seen it, he wouldn't have even considered if it might have been his beleaguered third platoon. He hadn't given one thought to their welfare since he sent them through the wire on that fateful evening. All that mattered was his own skin.

Pivoting at a right angle to the west, the pilot took his ship on a direct course to the 2d Battalion, 1st Marine Regiment's aid station. He'd received word that more wounded had arrived and that several serious cases needed immediate evacuation to the USS Repose located off the coast.

As the helicopter touched down, two sets of litter bearers raced to the open hatch and shoved the stretchers into the fuselage, knocking Captain Parker to the side as he tried to exit.

"Watch where the fuck you're going, assholes," he shouted above the roar of the rotor blades. The navy medical corpsmen ignored him and raced back to the aid station.

As Lester Parker slinked back to his tent, he noticed an unusual amount of activity around the battalion command post. He had no idea what might be happening and only wanted to return unnoticed to his company's area. When he arrived, he sought out his executive officer.

Things looked different, even though it was dark. He couldn't locate his tent and finally stumbled upon his radio operator. "Corporal Browning, where is Lieutenant Stewart?"

"He doesn't work here anymore Captain Parker and neither do you."

"Don't get fucking smart with me Corporal."

"I'm not sir. We have a new company commander and executive officer. They took over about two hours ago."

Confused and irate, Lester Parker had thought Lieutenant Colonel Flaherty would let things settle before he actually relieved him. He didn't expect him to act so swiftly; now it would be awkward for him to assume command again once General Walker had reinstated him.

Filled with confidence from his recent visit to division headquarters, Parker continued exercising his flawed judgment. Walking directly to the battalion commander's tent, he called in an assertive and hyperbolic tone, "Lieutenant Colonel Flaherty, I demand to speak with you immediately!"

At once, the battalion commander appeared at his tent flap. The moon's pale light reflected off his truculent and grizzled face. Its lines, accentuated by lack of sleep, made him appear as some prehistoric creature of questionable human origins.

Captain Parker became frightened by the spectacle before him and stood rigid in the presence of the man he was trying to bring down. He knew he'd met his match and for the first time sensed the battle was far from over.

"Do you understand English Captain Parker?" came a low, guttural, rhetorical question from the commander.

"What do you mean, sir?"

"I mean this, you sorry excuse for a human being: You pack your trash and report directly to regimental headquarters. Do not pass go; do not collect $200; just do it! Colonel Johnson will advise you of your new duties.

"You no longer work for me. I have relieved you of your command. You sicken me, and I want never to see you again. When things settle down enough for me to catch-up administratively, I will write you an unsatisfactory fitness report and prefer charges against you for dereliction of duty. And I hope it results in a court-martial for your prissy ass. You are a disgrace to the Marine Corps, and I'll do whatever it takes to destroy you. Do you understand?"

Captain Parker began to shake, his mouth twitching and his knees quivering as though he was about to initiate some silly dance. Suddenly he felt the warm sensation of urine running down his left leg and into his combat boot.

Lieutenant Colonel Flaherty returned inside his tent as quickly as he'd appeared, leaving the clownish figure standing in front of it, gawking into space, his eyes bulging and his face growing pale. Seconds later he fainted, falling forward through the tent flap and onto the deck of the battalion commander's tent.

The colonel, ignoring him, stepped over the prostrate officer and into the clear night air. He took a moment to gaze at the magnificent heavens. Off in the distance, several 105mm artillery flares lit the night skies and forced the harried officer back to the tasks at hand. He turned abruptly and headed for his command post and his anxious staff.

Moments later, Lester Parker regained consciousness. Alone and soiled, he rose to a partial sitting position, supported by his right arm. In the eerie light of the cramped tent, he witnessed a surrealist vision of his own mortal being. Thoughts of his known shortcomings, which he'd made every effort to suppress in the past, now overwhelmed his psyche. He finally saw himself as he really was.

The words of his wife were the first to enter his mind. She knew him better than anyone and the longer they'd lived together, the more she saw through him. One evening, after she'd caught him lying about a recent affair, she'd referred to him as a total phony. He'd vocally dismissed her words, but like all men, he stored them in his heart where they cut deeply. Communication is irreversible and her words would never leave him and he would never feel the same toward her nor her toward him. Fidelity had no meaning in their marriage, nor did it have meaning in his Marine life.

Lester Parker thought of the times in grade school that he had duped teachers and students alike. He recalled the same actions in high school and at VMI. By then, he'd become rather proficient at his toadyism and ceased to consider their moral correctness.

Now, the awfulness of his efforts to place the eminent loss of his third platoon on the shoulders of his commanding officer even struck him as revolting.

Captain Lester Parker rose to his feet and walked outside the tent. Drawing his .45 caliber pistol from his shoulder holster, he chambered a round and put the muzzle into his mouth.

When he pulled the trigger, the large projectile, generating 356 foot pounds of energy, splattered his brain stem, driving parts of it and surrounding bone fragments out the back of his head.

He collapsed in a heap, as feces and remnants of urine filled his trousers. Captain Parker instantly died an abhorrent death, befitting his duplicitous lifestyle.

The lone discharge alerted sentries and those close to the battalion command post. Lieutenant Colonel Flaherty had just entered the operations section when the shot went off. Immediately he thought that someone had accidentally cranked off a round. Such discharges did happen on occasion but were not tolerated. The battalion policy dealt with these incidents severely.

Angered by the thought of some loose cannon wandering around inside the perimeter, the battalion commander was about to direct someone to see what had happened when a wireman from the communications platoon ran inside the command center. In a hyped-up state, he blurted out to his platoon commander, 1st Lieutenant Fernandez, that Captain Parker had just shot himself.

Lieutenant Colonel Flaherty heard the report and threw back his head in disgust. Under his breath he mumbled, "The son-of-a-bitch didn't even have the balls to face the music."

He had a platoon in grave danger and now, in addition, he had to contend with one of his officers committing suicide.

"Put him in a body bag and drag him over to the battalion aid station where they can tag him. Let's devote all of our efforts to Golf Company's third platoon right now."

He turned to Major Wagner, his executive officer: "Norm, I want you to handle the investigation on Captain Parker. You'd best get started right away because his death will generate plenty of interest. Let's try and beat the heavies to the punch. I'll provide you a statement on my recent confrontation with him. In the interim, pull together the basics and oversee the death message. Division could make me a party to this thing. We'll just have to wait and see."

Major Wagner left the command bunker and Lieutenant Colonel Flaherty turned to his air liaison officer who'd started to brief him when Lester Parker shot himself.

"Sir, the Huey we sent out this afternoon, with Captain Sloan aboard, didn't return. They are way past their ETA. We've had no radio contact with them since they last reported said Captain Chuck Wilham, an A-4 attack pilot on exchange duty with Lieutenant Colonel Flaherty's battalion.

"What was their last message and where did they send it from?"

"Sir, from the battalion's old position and the third platoon was there. They were unloading supplies and fixing to depart. That's the last we heard. I don't know if they made it off or went down somewhere en route back here or what. Could be their radio went bad but we should have heard something by now."

"I don't like the smell of this one. Until we know what's going on back there, it's pretty hard to act.

"What I want you to do is lay on an aerial recon at first light. We've got Hotel Company on standby. Reconfirm arrangements for HMM 262 to be on standby too so they can transport Hotel over there to extract the third platoon, if it comes to that. Also make sure the air folks at regiment know we may need some fixed-wing close air support to complete the package. In the interim, I'll have the S-3 work up a frag order and we'll get all the wheels in motion. We've got enough to do up here without having to divert resources elsewhere, but we don't have any choice."

He gave his commander's guidance like an orchestra leader conducting his musicians. Knowing exactly what to do, all members of the battalion, in unison, commenced to execute the complex tasks at hand. The unit worked with incredible synergy; they had fought together for a long time and could count on each other. They had a mission, and they would carry it out with alacrity and precision. Everyone knew what to do, down to and including the hospital corpsman tagging Lester Parker's lifeless body.

CHAPTER 23

All the while Captain Parker was attempting to salvage his career, Ned O'Shea and his platoon were desperately trying to save themselves.

Ned had to contend with two things: He was now surrounded and he had to hold until morning when Captain Sloan said help might arrive. It was their only hope. Trying to breakout would only allow the NVA to pick them off piecemeal. If he could shrink his perimeter, rearrange his protective wire and inflict enough casualties on any probe or major attack, he might be able to buy time.

He called his squad leaders up, along with Sergeant Gilmore. Taking inventory, he found all his men were still functional. Two had sustained slight wounds in the mortar attack on the helicopter.

Fortunately, the battalion S-4 had included ample parachute flares, claymore mines, 10 LAWs, two machine guns and three starlight scopes when he put together a resupply package for Ned's platoon. Although hardly as effective as flares from a 60mm or 81mm mortar, the hand fired types provided sufficient illumination to spot targets. The platoon could hold them in reserve and pickup early movement with the three starlight scopes.

Besides the newly acquired items, Ned determined they had plenty of ammunition for the limited weapons they had. Aside from M-16 rifles, they still had the platoon's normal compliment of M-79 grenade launchers and hand grenades.

Continuing to harbor grave doubts about his platoon's ability to ward off a determined assault, he nevertheless felt a little reassured by the amount of firepower at his disposal. When the NVA hit, he would bloody them badly and hopefully cause them to await reinforcements before trying again.

His fire team leaders and Sergeant Gilmore looked at him with searching and anxious eyes. He knew they were placing all their hopes in his ability to save them from the crisis they faced. He could not let them down, yet he felt few of them would survive the ordeal.

Ned methodically told his subordinate leaders what their responsibilities would entail. As soon as it became dark, they would shrink their current lines and restring new protective wire that the battalion had left behind in neat stacks.

Between the new wire and that already in place, they would affix claymore mines. Ned figured that those NVA who did not detonate the personnel mines outside the old battalion perimeter and were not cut down breaching its protective wire, would face a metallic curtain thrown at them by the claymores. He'd hold his machine guns in reserve and deploy them only when he could determine where the main attack would strike. Their interlocking bands of chest-high fire would thwart any final attempt to reach his positions.

As the last rays of the sun shrunk from the mountains to their west, Ned and his men took a few sporadic AK-47 rifle rounds fired from distant points around their perimeter. Maybe Charlie just wanted to let them know he had them surrounded and was priming them for a big onslaught.

As quickly as the rest of the 2d Battalion 1st Marine Regiment prepared for battle, so did Ned and his men. Those not stringing wire worked on their fortifications, ensuring they had good fields of fire and plenty of cover. They could expect an abundance of mortar fire and possibly some artillery rounds too.

Shortly before midnight, preparations were completed and Ned returned to his foxhole and slid into it. Removing his helmet and then taking his canteen from its pouch, he lustily drank the tepid water and leaned back against the cool earth. Staring into the heavens, his thoughts drifted away from the conflict at hand and sought some metaphysical purpose for his presence. Like so many of his countrymen throughout history, he too had become one of the Wild Geese.

Ireland's young men, for centuries, fought wars in Europe and South America. Countries found the small island provided a ready source of good soldiers, a reputation which continued and became a sad part of the Irish heritage. Ned postulated that his ancestors too had found themselves subjugated and proscribed to a life of servitude at the hands of their English masters and the thought of escape and adventure proved too tempting for them. Out of need or want, they fled the island in droves and scattered themselves throughout the troubled spots of the earth. Few, if any, ever returned. Ned felt he was about to become one of these maudlin statistics.

Dismissing such morbid thoughts, he instead reflected on those persons who influenced his early life. It was the orphanage that came to mind and Sister Mary Carla who'd probably saved him. A large, happy woman, she provided him a warmth that he'd never known before nor since.

After he'd left for his university studies, she told him during a return visit that when the authorities brought him to Saint Brendan's Orphanage, he was undernourished and failing to thrive. She said he had gaunt eyes with a terrified look in them. At that point, she related how she dedicated herself to his well-being.

He remembered how he responded to her continuing warm, yet tough love. She would hold him and tell him stories and then again would not tolerate any foolishness, all the while laughing.

Ned also recalled, as senescence overtook her, their last conversation. A compulsive act drove him to call right before he escaped to America. When she came to the telephone, he identified himself, whereupon her frail and reedy, yet still jovial voice expressed how glad she was to hear from him; then she said, "Ned, I'm 85 years old and I still have all my own teeth." He remembered holding the receiver away from his face and looking at it, realizing Sister Mary Carla had never talked about herself and now she didn't know up from down. The ravages of old age had reduced her to a shell of her former self: a silly old woman no longer capable of the selflessness which had made her the powerful force she had been. Sadly, he'd asked her to pray for him and told her goodbye, knowing full well the minute she hung up she would have no recollection that she had even talked with him.

A sense of foreboding and terrible loneliness returned to him. Realizing he could very well be dead within the next eight hours, Ned felt unfulfilled. He'd never been close to anyone, never known the love of a woman nor the joy of a family. It seemed like hate filled his life, fueling his drive and not allowing him to appreciate so many of the finer aspects which a normal existence had to offer. As a young man, he broke treasured items in fits of anger. He became a man possessed with a compelling desire to kill and when he did, it troubled him not. Only this aspect made him wonder if he had all his marbles.

"Lieutenant," came a soft call from Sergeant Gilmore above Ned's fighting hole.

Startled from his contemplative mood, Ned quickly stood in a somewhat agitated state.

"What?" he tersely answered his platoon sergeant.

"Sir, I have a collective fire team and the section of machine guns in position by our command post as you directed. We're set to respond to any sector of the perimeter which might need reinforcements."

Realizing he'd ordered Sergeant Gilmore to do just that earlier in the evening, he felt a little embarrassed by his sharp reply.

"Thanks sergeant," came his second reply. "About all we can do now is wait for Charlie to make his move. I want all hands awake and ready on the line. I know he will hit us tonight; we've got to give him everything we've got if we hope to survive."

Ned could see the whites of Sergeant Gilmore's eyes. They were bulging, reflecting the desperation the young sergeant sensed in their predicament.

"Don't think about it Sergeant Gilmore; when it happens, throw yourself into it. The men need your steady hand. We'll prevail; have faith."

Sergeant Gilmore flashed a nervous smile. He knew his lieutenant read him like a book, yet he knew Ned loved him like a brother, despite his humanness.

As he left his platoon commander, he marveled at how the lieutenant made all the men feel the same way. Regardless of Marines rotating in and out of country and the platoon's ranks being depleted by casualties, the same synergy prevailed, whether a man was an old hand or a boot. Sergeant Gilmore had heard noncommissioned officers from other platoons speak in envy of those assigned to

Golf Company's 3d Platoon. Their reputation had become almost legendary within the battalion and everyone knew the fierce, distant and competent lieutenant generated it.

Sergeant Gilmore remembered before one particularly dicey operation, all the men were anxious. Gathered together in their assembly area, they waited for their lieutenant to return from the company command post with a frag order. Instead of methodically going over the platoon's scheme of maneuver, Ned began to talk about inconsequential things. The men didn't know how to react to his insouciant manner, and then they began to listen attentively as they sensed him effortlessly shifting gears into the task they faced. They hung on every word.

When all thought he had finished, he paused and began to speak of Winston Churchill, a man about whom most of the platoon knew nothing. He gave them a brief of this wartime leader, and then noted one of his sayings appropriate for their circumstances. Unrehearsed, the lieutenant softly spoke Churchill's words, "Death and sorrow will be the companions of our journey; hardship our garments; constancy and valor our only shield. We must be united, we must be undaunted, we must be inflexible."[1] It stuck and the men responded.

After the battle, Sergeant Gilmore approached Ned and asked if he would write down the words of Churchill that he had addressed to the platoon before they had gone

---

[1] Reproduced with permission of Curtis Brown, London on behalf of Sir Winston Churchill Copyright © Winston S. Churchill

into battle. He then committed them to memory. Although he never heard his lieutenant utter them again, he himself would repeat the words like a prayer in times of crisis. Now was no exception.

Sergeant Gilmore was not the only one who hung on Churchill's words. Five-hundred meters from the platoon's position, Major Au met with his company commanders. He had just completed a final mandate his officers would follow. They would take the Marine's position according to the plan he'd briefed them on earlier in the evening.

Although the moon was full, he felt confident a diversionary attack on the Marine's eastern flank would draw their attention from the jungle to the west from whence he would launch his major assault. One company would breach the wire and the other two would stream through and overwhelm the Marine defenders.

He told his subordinate commanders of a time when as a member of the Vietminh, fighting the French, Ho Chi Minh had addressed the officers in Au's regiment. Ho spoke of his politically formative years in France and Russia in the 1920s. Europe, and its rising socialist parties of the times, cultivated his nationalism and communistic philosophies. He became an ardent linguist, speaking Vietnamese, French, Russian, Chinese and English. He continued to read in all the languages and studied the great leaders of the century. He quoted Churchill, Mao and other war-time leaders who knew that victory came at all costs. And he imparted their messages to his officers, instilling in them the understand-ing that the road ahead would be long and cruel.

Major Au stared at his officers and then uttered in a rasping tone, "We will achieve victory, tonight, tomorrow and in the end we will prevail. Now return to your compa-nies. We will commence our attack at 0100."

At 0045, Lance Corporal Tim Hagerty squinted through his squad's starlight scope, looking east. The bright moon added to the ease with which he could see. Suddenly there was movement—what looked to be many camouflaged men crawling toward the platoon's position.

"Sergeant Piper, we've got gooks moving on us. Must be at least a platoon. They're about 300 meters out," the young Marine said in a confident yet resigned manner.

Without answering him, the squad leader dashed to Ned's position, located in the center of the platoon.

"Sir, we've got Charlie moving toward us from in front of my squad's position. We picked him up with the scope; he's about 300 meters from the wire."

Ned likewise said nothing and grabbing the platoon's sniper rifle, darted to the threatened area with Sergeant Piper close behind.

The two Marines immediately dropped into Sergeant Piper's foxhole. Peering through the scope on his rifle, Ned could readily make out the vestige of men on the move.

"Pass the word for your men to hold fire. I think this is just a probe. The main thrust will come from somewhere else. Right now I'm going to see if I can force them to commit themselves prematurely."

Knowing his platoon would not fire unless directed to do so, Ned eased the rifle into his shoulder and sighted on an easy, slow-moving target. The round was down range in an instant and the target convulsed wildly for a moment and then was silent.

The others heard the shot and began to crawl faster. With another round chambered, Ned sent the projectile racing toward a second target. It hit in an instant and the NVA soldier let out a horrible scream. Another shot found its target a moment later and the predicted outcome came to pass.

The entire NVA platoon rose and started to charge the first squad's positions. Before moving 25 meters, they hit a mine field. Antipersonnel mines, in the form of Bouncing Betties, erupted from their internments and tore into the attackers. The men of the first squad watched in terrified amazement as the onslaught unfolded before them.

Firing wildly, only four men from the entire NVA platoon made it to the first strand of wire. Those designated to breach the wire were already dead and when the four hit the razor sharp strands, they simply became ensnared. Ned shot each of them as they struggled in vain to free themselves.

The entire probe was over in minutes; the only remnants remaining were four bodies hanging grotesquely in front of the Marine position.

Ned ran back to his command post in the center of his platoon and called his squad leaders up. When they had reached him, he quickly told them to expect a major attack from another sector within the perimeter and to have all hands ready to repel it. The subordinate leaders scurried back to their respective squads, passed the word and waited.

Major Au became confused. It appeared the diversionary force had initiated its attack too soon and upset his timetable. He was unaware of the disaster which struck the platoon. He'd only heard a few shots, then explosions and AK-47 rifle fire. But they were 15 minutes early.

He ordered the two companies who were to make the primary assault to commence their attack. They had not arrived at their designated release points when word reached the lead company to form a skirmish line and charge the Marines' position.

Major Au knew better but his impulsive nature demanded immediate results. He hoped he had not lost the element of surprise as far as his main attack was concerned. Possibly the Marines were absorbed with the actions on their eastern perimeter and were unprepared for the major thrust he was about to deliver them.

His lead company was to hastily breech the protective wire and the follow-on company would pass through them and fan out inside the Marines' perimeter. Each platoon would then attack a pie-shaped sector.

But it didn't happen that way.

Ned's squad on the west side of the perimeter peering through a starlight scope picked up massive movement to their front. The squad leader, Sergeant Bill Langley, called out, "Here they come Lieutenant," while simultaneously firing a parachute flare.

Hoping to seize the moment, Major Au's initial attacking force found themselves illuminated by a small angling flare. They were on line and 200 meters from their objective.

Ned dispatched his machine guns to Sergeant Langley's squad and launched a green star cluster signaling the platoon to fire its final protective fires. Two more parachute flares popped above the attacking NVA company as the Marines commenced to fire into their midst. Two hundred and fifty well aimed shots per minute erupted from Sergeant Langley's men. M-79 grenade launchers and LAWs vomited their deadly projectiles into the North Vietnamese. Coupled with the interlocking bands of machine gun and M-16 rifle fire, the scene became chaotic. Even at night, the NVA were easy targets. Many of them reached the outer wire but were butchered as they bunched up, attempting to breech the concertina.

Major Au had the sense to stop his second company from following in trace of the attacking soldiers. He watched helplessly as his lead elements became statistics.

Ned's Marines cut Major Au's attacking force to ribbons. Determined and mission oriented, most of the NVA continued their forward movement, only to die quickly or in some agonizingly slow way. Besides the high velocity projectiles ripping into their ranks, the shell fragments from the exploding grenades and rockets only added to the nightmare. Men saw torsos disappear in front of them, and then suffer the same fate moments later.

Despite all the carnage, Major Au's troops did two important things. They placed bangalore torpedoes under the protective wire and detonated them.

The shredded concertina reached into the air and separated. A gaping hole resulted and six NVA soldiers scurried through the opening. Three of them actually reached the second ring of wire before Ned's men mowed them down.

Realizing they'd ceased to exist as a fighting force, remnants of the attacking company struggled back to their point of departure. Most of the company lie strewn in front of Sergeant Langley's squad. Just 21 men of the 100 who jumped off in the attack made it to safety. Some cried while others simply collapsed. And the rest walked catatonically among the anxious reserves.

Undeterred, Major Au was already thinking of his next assault. He grabbed his retreating company commander and quickly assessed from him any positive aspects of the attack. Realizing his men had opened the protective wire, he saw his chance.

He also knew the Marine perimeter was small. The protective wire, strung in two elements, told him the shrunken boundary had to house no more than a platoon. And from the casualties he'd taken, he knew he confronted a savvy leader.

While Major Au regrouped his forces, Ned O'Shea did the same. Scurrying from squad to squad, he took casualty reports and passed words of encouragement and direction to his tired, yet resilient force. He felt great pride in his men and could not constrain the waves of emotion which spewed forth when he spoke to them. They in turn sensed his pride and smiled back in marked adulation. Their confidence intact, Ned left his men and returned to his command post. There Sergeant Gilmore sat, having just come back from making sure the right guide had resupplied all the men with ammunition, food and water.

"We took one KIA and three WIAs in that last attack Lieutenant," Sergeant Gilmore blurted out when Ned jumped into their foxhole.

"Yes, I know Sergeant Gilmore. Too bad the KIA is Sergeant Langley. He went to the aid of one of his men and some of the NVA must have seen him because they zapped him half a dozen times. He was dead before he hit the deck. The three WIAs were in his squad too. I'm going to reinforce his squad with a fire team each from our two other squads. I think the next attack will come from the same direction, if it comes at all. And I want you to take over the squad, Sergeant Gilmore."

The sergeant's eyes widened and after a long pause he softly said, "Aye-aye sir."

Somehow, sensing his time on this planet was about to end, Sergeant Gilmore began to confide in his lieutenant. Needing to expunge the thoughts agonizing his tortured soul, he didn't ask his officer if he could talk about something other than the crisis at hand; he just began to speak in low and rapid tones.

"Sir, before the Corps sent me here to Nam, they put me aboard the USS Coronado, an LPD in Morehead City, North Carolina and we sailed east and bored holes in the Mediterranean Sea for six months as part of some amphibious ready group with the 6th Fleet. Three months before we set sail, my wife delivered our son, Gregory Gilmore.

"Sir, I'd never been happier in my life. He was the grandest little fellow you'd ever want to see. He was my son and I was so proud of him.

"Out in the Med, my wife would send me pictures of him, tell me how much he was changing, how she truly loved me and couldn't wait until I got home and all that shit.

"I really loved her too, lieutenant and when the ship reached the states, I nearly pole vaulted down the gangway, only to find her nowhere in sight.

"As I stood there with a confused look on my face, some Navy chaplain asked if I was Sergeant Gilmore. I nodded and then he dumped a load of shit on me that you wouldn't believe.

"According to him, my darling wife was making it with some 2d Class Navy Corpsman she'd met when she took our son to the hospital there on the base at Camp Lejeune; she'd subsequently filed for divorce. I found out later, she'd maxed out our credit cards and blown what little savings we had.

"I saw them in the PX two days later and lost it; pointing to my wife, I asked lover boy how he liked screwing the bitch?

"He flipped me off, and I decked his ass right there in the checkout line.

"My old lady screamed and the MPs had me in cuffs before I knew what happened. After that, the Corps gave me one of two options--volunteer for Nam right then or face a court-martial.

"Anyway, here I am sir and I don't know if I'll ever see my son again!

"I feel like a cross between Edward Hopper and Vincent Van Gogh; I'm one of those melancholy figures Hopper painted...always alone! And Van Gogh, he never fit either. Constantly around others but still alone, he ended up shooting himself in the balls and died three days later. The Corps is the only family I've got!"

Sergeant Gilmore bit into his lower lip and felt a flood of tears suddenly spill from his tired and salt encrusted eyes.

Ned knew his sergeant well. He was not the ordinary, uneducated NCO but rather had an Associate Arts degree in commercial art. Knowing the draft was about to take him, he enlisted and had done quite well in a short time. He was like any young stallion though, always chomping at the bit and in high gear.

Ned never spoke and finally the emotionally drained sergeant turned his head slowly and looked at his leader. He saw him through the eyes of an artisan. The ominous night shadows cast a foreboding reflection off the lieutenant's face. It approximated what Captain Parker saw in his vision of Lieutenant Colonel Flaherty, only there was a difference. Beneath these austere and muddy tones appeared a smile.

Sergeant Gilmore had never seen anything like it. The smile was classic, like a masculine Mona Lisa; its surrealistic composure seemed to freeze time. It conveyed a message stronger than any words and its intent was one of warmth, reassurance and compassion. It said, "I understand and accept you without conditions."

Fighting to regain his composure, Sergeant Gilmore said, "I'll go down now and check on my squad, lieutenant."

He put his elbows on the lip of the foxhole and lifted himself up and threw one leg over the top, then rolled over. He left his lieutenant, never to see him again and moved slowly in a hunched position toward the edge of the perimeter, feeling like he'd seen an apparition.

CHAPTER 24

The clear, warm and calm night seemed like an eternity for the men of Ned's platoon. They continued to scan their front but saw nothing. Only the doleful moans of several severely wounded NVA soldiers, lying somewhere in the bush, punctuated the still air.

As night wore on, Ned began to sense a terrible natural phenomenon enveloping both his men and his position. The warm air rising from the earth began to cool by conduction. He'd seen it before, and he couldn't think of a worse time for it to happen...radiation fog!

All at once he felt helpless...a premonition of what might be in store for all of them. Anxiously he watched as the outlines of his men faded into the enveloping mist. Soon he could see nothing. They were totally socked in, like he'd seen on the coast of Ireland. He couldn't communicate with his men or they with him.

As Ned disparaged, Major Au became ebullient. Like a gift from the gods, he realized the cosmos had presented him with a totally unexpected opportunity.

Long in the tooth, he flashed a tusky smile as he called for his company commanders. He quickly briefed them on his course of action. He would employ primarily three of the nine principles of war...surprise, simplicity and mass.

The fog would provide for his surprise; the direct route through the Marines' lines would make for simplicity and the mass of his force, coupled with a heavy mortar barrage, would overwhelm the defendants.

Anticipating such a formidable encounter, Major Au had positioned his 82mm mortars so as to provide the massing of fires. The four tubes, fixed in place 200 meters behind his front lines, were sighted in on the Marine perimeter from the previous shelling of the helicopter. Each man in his battalion carried two mortar rounds and they had deposited them with the tubes in preparation for the attack. With over 800 rounds at their disposal, the mortar men felt highly charged and confident.

Major Au's attack plan unfolded with alacrity. He'd shot an azimuth to the point where the outer wire had been breached prior to the fog descending. He would send his attached sappers with bangalore torpedoes forward to the final protective wire. Along the route they would run engineer tape to guide his attacking companies. Once the mortar barrage started, the engineers would slink up to the wire and push the torpedoes under it. The mortar rounds would mask the explosions in the wire and the Marines, not knowing his men had breached the concertina, wouldn't be able to respond in time to stop his superior force.

Major Au felt confident and determined. This time his battalion would prevail. The small element of Marines had shamed him as they had both detected and cut down his previous attacks. He sensed his men questioned his leadership because of his impulsive and dominant style and the terrible losses they'd recently suffered. He'd heard grumblings, but knew all that would fade when they took the Marines' position; nothing enhanced morale more than victory.

Major Au's battalion began to move. It resembled a locomotive straining to overcome inertia as the men fumbled and stumbled, gathering their assault equipment and making ready for the uphill struggle.

Surprisingly, they were positioned within short order. Anxious and fixed, the force resembled a coiled spring, ready to unleash its energy against any resistance in its way. Nervous energy alone kept the exhausted men from falling asleep as they strained their eyes and awaited the first sounds of the attack.

As they knelt, facing their front, they heard in the distance a voice. The language was English but they couldn't understand it. What it did tell them was the Americans were alert, at least some of them.

The voice was that of Ned O'Shea. Crying aloud to his men in desperation, he exhorted them to remain alert, telling them the fog had given the NVA a window of opportunity and that they had to hold at all costs. Help was only hours away. His squad leaders echoed his orders but they too could not be sure their men remained at the ready.

Ned's men were more exhausted than the NVA. Somehow the fog had covered them like a veil of solace; they felt secure and relaxed. Despite their lieutenant's and squad leaders' implorings, a third of the men could not remain awake. They fell asleep in varied positions. Giving into the body's demand for reprieve, they slipped into a quiet stupor, much like a driver falling asleep at the wheel.

Ned gritted his teeth. He hated not having total control of any situation but this had to be the worst. He'd experienced terrible confrontations before, but he always knew what to do. He could draw from multiple assets at his disposal. At times it was artillery; other times he called in close air support. The Corps consistently operated like a well oiled mechanism in combat. Things happened with precision and they would inevitably gain the upper hand. Between the efficiency of the killing machine and the élan of the troops, Ned had an unbeatable combination. But now, certain ingredients were missing. Captain Parker, he felt, had dealt him a fatal hand. Exposed, short-handed and lacking communications, Ned knew the odds favored neither him nor his men.

He felt a wave of melancholia sweep over him as he stared into the impenetrable curtain of fog. Never before had Ned experienced this kind of fear. The obscure setting detached him from the usual reality with which he could deal. Seemingly suspended in time and eternity, he thought of death and the awfulness of perishing in the remoteness of Vietnam. He reflected again on Ireland and his own lack of fulfillment. There seemed to be little normalcy in his life. Even from his early childhood, the road before him offered little peace or reason. He'd gone from one crisis to another and finally graduated into the status of a mercenary. He was nothing more. Like so many of his ancestors, he faced the terrible reality of death for a cause for which he neither understood nor cared. He was only proficient at what he did best and that was waging war.

An intense anger replaced his trepidation, and he resolved to hold on and lead his men to safety when the fog dissipated.

His drifting thoughts ceased when he heard the muted pops of what sounded like Champaign bottles uncorked in a distant room. He knew them to be mortar rounds tubed by the gun crews and heading for his position.

Within seconds, the vaulting projectiles began exploding inside Ned's perimeter. He had no worries about his men sleeping now. Each one knew the fateful moment had arrived. This was the harbinger of their walk with death. How many would survive and what kind of carnage awaited those selected ones, no one knew.

Like animals, their instincts took over and they hugged the earth, hoping to become one with it. The lower they positioned themselves, the better chance they had of avoiding the shell fragments bursting up and away from their points of impact. Some of the newer men cried and shook with fear. The salty veterans shared their fear but overcame the shock with resigned determination. If they could live through the barrage, they had hope of surviving another hour or day. Such was the ethos of the infantryman. He lived a simple but terrifying life and the terror was now upon him in spades.

Ned's eyes darted about his perimeter but he could see nothing but periodic flashes from the bursting mortar rounds. As he was lowering his head, a sudden explosion on the edge of his position struck his head and upper body. The blast tore off his helmet and jagged pieces of hot metal ripped into the soft tissues of his back, neck and portions of his skull. Everything went black and he slumped to the bottom of his fighting hole along with mounds of earth which caved into its bottom.

As Ned lie motionless, far to the north, Lieutenant Colonel Flaherty angrily set the wheels in motion to extract Ned and his men. Disgusted by the stupidity and cowardice of Captain Parker, the battalion commander seemed obsessed by the need to save the beleaguered platoon.

The tension in the combat operations center reached a critical point as staff officers keyed radio sets and passed warning orders to elements within and outside the battalion.

Pulling his Air Liaison Officer aside, Lieutenant Colonel Flaherty spoke to him in simple and direct terms.

"Chuck, is everything set with the air folks; can they support us?"

"Yes sir, everything is set. We have an OV-10 fragged to recon the old CP as soon as he's cleared for VFR," came the response from the seasoned attack pilot. He was more at home pulling on the pole in the cockpit of an A-4 attack jet and had resisted his transfer to an infantry battalion. But the time he spent with the "grunts" had changed his whole perspective of the Corps. No longer narrow in focus, he saw the coordination needed for the air/ground team to work. Down deep, he had come to feel comfortable with the infantry, something some of his immature contemporaries never experienced. They arrived at such assignments bitter and left the same way, only with their careers in ruin because groovy fellows didn't fare well in the trenches.

Slowly the fog began to dissipate as the sun rose and burned off the air's heavy laden moisture. At the same time, a Marine OV-10 pilot pushed the throttles forward on his twin engine aircraft as it sped down Runway 34 at Quang Tri's airfield. Darting off the surface well before the 3,000 foot mark, it swiftly climbed out and headed for the map coordinates of the 2d Battalion's old position.

Meanwhile, Major Au troops had overrun Ned's platoon, and the major now savored a victory which heretofore he had never known. Although somewhat minor compared to major offenses he'd experienced in the past, this one had a ring of ardor. He had systematically eliminated the Marines' chances for escape and overwhelmed them in a tactical display of brilliance. Aggressive and persistent, he had vanquished a resilient force; one which he considered more than a worthy opponent.

He stood with his executive officer and two of his company commanders at the center of the 2d Battalion,1st Marine Regiment's abandoned command post and now the graveyard of one of its platoons. His men were systematically checking all positions within its perimeter and executing any wounded survivors.

Major Au, animated and flushed with excitement, euphorically reviewed the masterful stroke which brought them victory. His subordinate officers grinned with approval and joined in the melodic chatter of their conquest. They had but a short time to savor their glory prior to heading east to sever Route 1 and render more havoc among the Marine forces. So they let their guard down and drank in the intoxicating moment at hand.

As their sing-song verbiage punctuated the lifting fog, Ned O'Shea, covered with blood and debris, began to sense consciousness. At first, the harmonious tones of the Vietnamese language made him think he had entered some visionary state as he had no comprehension of his injuries or the peril around him. But slowly the radiant heat of the sun and the throbbing pain in his upper body and head jolted him into reality.

Immediately he knew the enemy stood over him and they had overrun both him and his men. Instinctively, he slowly moved his right hand in search of his pistol. It had fallen between his legs when he sustained the mortar wounds and had lain shielded from the rubble which covered him.

The pain became overwhelming but lessened when his fingers felt the cool steel of his weapon's receiver. He knew he had the pistol cocked and had a round chambered; he only had to flick off the safety to arm it.

He could taste the alien warmth of his own blood as it ran down his face and into his mouth. He assumed the NVA had taken him for dead and had bypassed him for more promising kills. Blinking deliberately, he cleared his vision and looked upward. The misty images before him soon came into focus and he instinctively riveted on the NVA officers above him.

Major Au stood in the middle, dominating the dialogue. His sinister and incredibly grotesque smile told Ned this was the prince of darkness incarnate who had terrorized his platoon over the past 12 hours.

Somehow sensing his actions would be his last, he gathered every element of strength his fractured body could muster and rose like a modern day phoenix from the bottom of his foxhole. Instinctively, his arms brought the .45 caliber pistol directly away from his body as he rose; he clicked off the thumb safety and leveled the simple instrument of death directly at Major Au's head.

Before he could react, the NVA battalion commander found himself staring into a pistol barrel and, at the same instant, saw a spontaneous flash.

.45 caliber ammunition is particularly deadly. The bullet is large...230 grains; it travels at a relatively slow speed...835 feet per second. And its impact at close range is crushing.

The bullet hit Major Au squarely on the bridge of his nose and exploded out the back of his head, taking his pith helmet with it. He fell backwards, dying instantly.

Before his body struck the earth, Ned had cranked off three more rounds, killing the executive officer and the two company commanders. The executive officer took a bullet in the neck and both company commanders died of wounds to the thorax.

The exertion proved too much for Ned. Everything became fuzzy and faded into darkness as shock overwhelmed his anemic state. He pitched forward, face down in his foxhole.

An NVA soldier, reacting to the foreign sound of Ned's .45 caliber pistol, ran to the lip of the fighting hole and with his AK-47 rifle on full automatic, emptied its magazine into the fallen lieutenant's back.

The next senior officer in the 2d Battalion, 304th NVA Regiment was Captain Tung who Major Au had sent to the rear prior to the assault. Several confused lieutenants, who had survived the previous assaults, looked about for direction but found none forthcoming.

As the battalion faced a leadership crisis, the buzzing sound of a Marine OV-10 interrupted the now silent hilltop. Soldiers exchanged anxious glances; finally a call came for the battalion's attached 12.7mm Soviet M1938 heavy machine guns. They had remained with the mortars to the west of the position but the gunners heard the shrieking pitch too and trained their sights on the fast approaching aircraft.

Coming from the east out of the sun, the swift twin engine plane darted over the northern end of the perimeter and banked hard to the north, leaving little chance for the gunners to fire any accurate shots. Several bursts of errant rounds punctuated the sky but were well off the mark.

The observer in the OV-10 had primed himself for the quick transit over the beleaguered position. As the plane headed north and gained altitude, he radioed back to the Lieutenant Colonel Flaherty's battalion operations center.

"Cedar Bird Three, this is Searchlight Tango: Do you read me? Over."

"Roger Searchlight Tango, this is Cedar Bird Three; we have you loud and clear...over."

"Roger Cedar Bird Three, this is Searchlight Tango; report large NVA force, estimated battalion size at coordinates 674283; no sign of friendlies...over."

"Roger Tango, understand NVA on position in mass and no sign of friendlies; wait...out."

The operations officer put his radio handset down and went over to his battalion commander who stood just outside the operations tent, talking with his executive office, the company commander of Hotel Company and the air liaison officer.

"Sir, we just heard from the OV-10 over our old position."

The tired and exasperated commander looked at his operations office with a faint glimmer of hope. Before the S-3 could relate what he'd heard, Lieutenant Colonel Flarerty spoke.

"Give it to me straight," as if he'd expected anything different.

"Sir, the aerial recon reports NVA all over the position and no sign of friendlies."

Everyone stood mute as the battalion commander clinched his fists and did all in his power to restrain an outburst.

Exhaling loudly, and then pausing for a moment, he said to his air liaison officer, "Do we have any air on station? If so, I want to pound those NVA bastards."

"Sir, I can check quickly, but we should have close to a squadron of A-4s on call in our sector waiting for targets of opportunity."

"Turn them over to the OV-10 and have him direct the air strike. In the interim, lets prepare to launch the CH-46s with our assault company into the area right after the A-4s have done their deed. We can have the OV-10 vector them in too."

"Aye-aye, sir," came the air officer's response.

The eclectic force quickly began to jell. Word went out to the various command and control elements of both the ground and air elements. Fortunately, six planes from an attack squadron at Chu Lai, to the south, had gotten airborne minutes before and were streaking north to support ground elements in need. The remainder of the squadron, six more planes, prepared to launch 15 minutes later.

Just north and west of Da Nang, the flight leader received word from the OV-10.

"Strike Victor, this is Searchlight Tango. Have approximate NVA battalion located coordinates 674283. Need immediate assistance. Will mark target with Willie Peter. Can you assist?"

"Roger Searchlight Tango, this is Strike Victor. Wilco. Anticipate be on station in zero-five minutes. Altitude two-eight-zero-zero. Loaded with daisy cutters and napalm. Request direction you want us to make our run. Suggest east to west if agreeable."

"Strike Victor, roger your last. East to west an affirmative. Will make my marking run north to south. Will time it when I have you overhead. Good luck. Searchlight Tango out."

As the A-4s flew to the east of the target area, Second Battalion troops embarked on helicopters at the battalion landing zone. Briefed on their mission and carrying full compliments of ammunition, an air of expectation appeared etched on all the Marines' faces. They anticipated the worst, meaning the NVA might shoot down some of the transports. It had happened on previous operation only weeks before. From boredom to terror, the cycle never seemed to change.

The leaderless NVA battalion remained perplexed. They heard the usual sounds of aircraft in the distance, but did not consider the possibility of an air strike on their position, especially this soon. The OV-10 had left after one pass and no one paid particular attention to it after that. The micromanagement of Major Au had anesthetized them to taking any immediate initiative.

Several lieutenants began to speak with each other, having received the word that the command elements died at the hand of one Marine. They commenced to debate whether to dig in their present position, form-up and move east to Route 1 or return to the regimental assembly area. They took too long.

Their troops, still milling around the dead Marines and stripping them of any booty worth collecting, failed to appreciate what was about to happen. Suddenly, the OV-10's whine increased and therewith came the sound of launching rockets. Before they could dive for cover, a series of white phosphorus rockets exploded within the perimeter.

Instinctively, they took cover and waited. Some weren't sure if artillery, mortars or what had fallen on them. Whatever, they sought the safety of the already dug trenches.

The heavy machine guns again barked at the low flying observation craft, only this time it presented a more viable target. Leading the plane with just enough space, the gunners felt confident as they let fly a hail of bullets. Collectively, they let out high pitched squeals as they saw smoke suddenly erupt from the aircraft's starboard engine. Almost as quickly, fire engulfed the wing and bits of metal began to sheer off. The right wing lost lift and the OV-10 drastically banked to the right and spun into the earth 300 feet below and 800 meters south of the objective. It exploded in a fireball which brought the NVA troops from their foxholes, cheering and knowing it was their day. They were invincible.

High above and to the east, the six A-4 attack jets circled in a lazy orbit at 10,000 feet. Lieutenant Colonel Pat McIver led the formation and keyed his mike. "Strike Victor, this is Strike Victor Leader. Searchlight Tango just bought the farm, but he marked the target. Disregard the burning wreckage to the south. We'll commence our attack east to west with high angle of attack for birds one through four. Birds five and six will make napalm drops on north south and east west runs. Let's do it."

Fixing on the burning white phosphorus, the leader's plane made the critical first dive, releasing six daisy cutters at 3,000 feet. He quickly leveled out and screeched low over the jungle canopy below. The bombs fell among the stunned NVA soldiers, who moments before were in jubilation.

The long fuses on the 250 pound bombs detonated the deadly instruments several feet off the deck. The fragments, instead of creating an enormous hole in the earth, flew about the perimeter with incredible velocity. Like a giant scimitar, the bombs cut down anything standing above ground.

Almost surgical in their precision, the jagged fragments tore into the fixated NVA soldiers. Those unfortunate ones, who did not find shelter in a foxhole, became anatomy lessons for the living. Every type of full scale vertical and horizontal anatomical cross-section imaginable appeared at that moment. Some died instantly while others screamed and moaned in mortal pain and terror.

The killing went on as the subsequent planes dropped their lethal loads. Those soldiers who tried to run away to the west suffered the same fate as those in the abandoned position.

The ones who hid in the foxholes sustained an equally terrifying fate. As they cowered at the bottom of the trenches, the last two A-4s pickled their napalm canisters which sucked up every bit of oxygen within the perimeter. The napalm's overwhelming heat and flames consumed the remaining components of the enemy battalion, even the mortar and heavy machine gun crews to the west of the position. One of the napalm canisters went long and landed in the middle of the gun crews. It fried everyone.

Fate had indiscriminately disposed two proud combat elements. Ned O'Shea and his men died in a valiant attempt to rejoin their unit. Overcome by the principle of mass, they did not have the wherewithal to hold out. Their self-serving and jealous commanding officer had resigned them to a cruel fate. Major Au's battalion left itself exposed to forces far beyond its ability to counter. Over-supervised and lacking leadership in the end, they failed to recognize or respond to the aerial danger which abruptly engulfed them.

The remaining hours of that morning seemed mechanical. The second flight of A-4s arrived on station and systematically bombed to the west of the now desolate perimeter. Their bombs and napalm struck among remaining elements of the NVA's 304th Regiment and hastened their retreat into the mountains to the west.

Lieutenant Colonel Flaherty's reaction force landed shortly thereafter and found the perimeter deserted, except for mangled and burned bodies. They took pains to identify their fallen comrades of the 3d Platoon and place their remains into body bags. The battalion S-4 arranged for a Ch-53 helicopter to transport the dead Marines to the graves registration platoon in Da Nang.

Before boarding awaiting CH-46 helicopters for the flight back to their northern positions, the reaction force looked for booty among the NVA corpses. It seems all combat men react the same.

EPILOGUE

The Vietnam Veterans of the First Marine Regiment held a small reunion in Washington D.C. on November 10, 1992, the date of the Marine Corps birthday.

The active duty elements of the Marine Corps were holding their formal birthday celebrations at major command locations throughout the world. A new breed, most had never served in Vietnam. Their only knowledge of the war came from a few crusty veterans or their required Marine Corps history and tradition classes.

All of the First Marine Regiment's reunion attendees had either retired from the Corps or left active service after one enlistment. About 250 made the trip. The men, for the most part, wore melancholy expressions. Their subdued rapport with their fellow Marines reflected only what they had collectively experienced, both before and after the war. Many had trouble adjusting to their surroundings when they returned home. They readily allowed that their fellow countrymen cared little about the Vietnam cause or their contribution to it. Just days earlier, those same countrymen had served them a final insult by electing a Vietnam draft dodger as president. The men carried this affront with resignation. Still it angered them.

Those who arranged the small reunion invited Major General Walker as their guest-of-honor. He'd wanted to decline due to poor health, but he accepted anyway. Prostate cancer had ravaged his body. He had lost considerable weight and tired easily. However, he felt he owed it to his old comrades to come. The general too suffered the melancholia which infected so many of his subordinates of the time. He could never shake the disappointment he had in the American people of the Vietnam era. Like Lyndon Johnson, he, too, retired to his home, only on the Outer Banks of North Carolina. He seldom ventured away from it or interacted with others. He drank too much and spent long hours plodding the beach or just looking out to sea. He had yet to reconcile that any useful purpose came from the carnage of Vietnam. He saw a fractured and cynical nation to which honor had no meaning and the likes of himself only represented the folly of the old fool. He would spontaneously sob for no apparent reason, and his wife remained perplexed by his suffering—something he could never share with her.

Colonel Jason Davis, now long retired, accepted an invitation to be the master of ceremonies for the dinner held in the compact motel dining room. The night before, members gathered for a happy hour and sea stories. Many paired up and went to eat at different ethnic restaurants within the city. The next day they toured the nation's capitol and thoroughly enjoyed the change of pace from the routine back home.

The reunion activities remained subdued. The dinner the evening of the 10th would be the major event. The next morning, those who wanted would lay a wreath at the Vietnam Memorial.

Colonel Davis sat next to General Walker. They exchanged small talk during dinner. Colonel Davis knew the general was ailing badly. He picked at his food and his hands shook when he tried to feed himself. His wife attended to him dutifully and darting looks of concern shot from her eyes at times when the general's feeble actions made him seem so out of place.

Sensing he'd best move the program along, Colonel Davis decided to introduce General Walker before everyone had finished eating. He rose and addressed the guests.

"Fellow Marines: We all share a common heritage; we served in Vietnam together. We shared an experience that except for the Wall, will most probably receive little thought as the passing years render it a footnote in this nation's history. But there are lessons our nation can possibly learn from our service. What they are I'm not certain, but it would be a shame if something positive did not come from it.

"We've asked General Walker to address us this evening. He fought in three wars. Wounded on Guadacanal and again on Iwo Jima, he clashed for four years in the Pacific in World War II as a platoon commander and company commander.

"He landed at Pusan, Korea in 1950 as a battalion commander and fought with the First Marine Brigade there. Later, he made the amphibious assault on Inchon and subsequently battled his way out of the Chosin Reservoir.

"Some of you may remember, he commanded the First Marine Division in Vietnam while a number of us were there.

"Let's all give a warm welcome to a distinguished Marine, Major General William Walker."

All hands stood and applauded the general as he slowly stood and moved to the lectern. He took some papers from his suit coat and placed them in front of him. Then he looked at the men's expectant faces. They charged him, and he felt comfortable around them. He hadn't experienced this sensation since he'd retired 22 years earlier.

"Thank you, Colonel Davis, for your kind introduction and for inviting me to address these fine Marines. I miss Marines. You are a breed all your own, and you brought me great joy in the years I served with you.

"Traditionally, remarks at reunions and on Marine Corps birthdays are short, and being a traditionalist, I will keep mine short, too.

"I struggled as to what I would say this evening. I ended up at a loss almost to the time my wife and I departed for Washington. But then I remembered an Army classmate of mine at the National War College. Some weeks ago, he'd mailed me a wonderful speech given by one of his colonels to a reunion of the First Brigade of the 101st Airborne Division. The good colonel is far more articulate than I am, but I believe his words speak for all those who fought in Vietnam. Let me share some of his poignant thoughts:

'It was 38 years ago that the exhausted remnants of a valiant French fighting force, covered with the blood and filth of battle, saw their national colors fall into the dirt at a place called Dien Bien Phu.

'For 54 days they held on, by holding on to one another. And by holding on to one another, they renewed their courage and faith until that too drained out of them like a lantern fading on dying batteries.

'Fifteen thousand dead, wounded, prisoners of war or missing in action.

'A continent away, no one cared. The contemporaries of the men under siege at Dien Bien Phu jammed the streets of Paris with demonstrations and angry protests. The joyous, grateful spirit of a people liberated from the Nazis just 10 years earlier had now withered and was covered with the scabs of indifference.

'The contempt of their countrymen notwithstanding, the Legionnaires struggled to do what their government had asked them to do at a place called Dien Bien Phu, 200 miles west of Hanoi.

'They captured their feelings for their struggle on a sign at the entrance to their cemetery—one found at other locations throughout Vietnam.

Stranger, if you journey into the land of the Spartans, tell them we lie here, obedient to their laws.

'Obedience.

'Pride in one's country, what it means, what it stands for.

'The sun set on the French at Dien Bien Phu. It rose on the United States.

'The baton was passed. History readied to repeat itself.

'The American people never understood that. The journalists who covered the war never understood that. The best and the brightest on our college campuses never understood that. And some, who simply should have known better, didn't.

'Maybe that is why some people are still struggling with the Vietnam question. Maybe now a generation later, our national conscience has a gnawing feeling that a critical piece is missing from the mosaic of their being.

'Maybe that is why the Vietnam Memorial is the most visited of all sites in the nation's capitol.

'Maybe.

'Maybe as they look at the wall with more than 50,000 neatly chiseled names, they ask questions they too cannot answer. And perhaps amidst the silence, tears and the muffled sound of shuffling feet, they understand the sense of the larger answer framed by a comrade in arms more than 40 years ago.

If you travel into the land of the Spartans, tell them we lie here, obedient to their laws.

'Obedience.

'Pride.

'Some inner force that has to be reckoned with and knowing that if you don't do it, you somehow are less than whole cloth.'

General Walker lowered his head and there was silence in the room.

The old gentleman, his eyes moistened, struggled to add a closing to the author's words.

"Men of the First Marines, you are of whole cloth. It matters not if you collect garbage, sweep streets, or make millions; you have your honor. You did not cut and run when others did.

"They saw you as chumps, but I dare say, to this day, they worry about their manhood."

General Walker, still earthy in his observations of life, knew his men and his thoughts translated well.

"May God bless every one of you and your families. Only from you will the fabric of a whole nation develop. Fortunately, there are enough of you who returned that can pass on the pride and obedience to your offspring that this nation so desperately needs."

His unsteady legs carried him to his seat as he heard spontaneous applause and a chorus of "Semper Fi" from his Marines...and he felt blessed.

The traditional birthday cake was cut. Everyone received a piece. Then members of the First Marines drifted off to party rooms to drink beer, tell lies and enjoy the camaraderie of their friends.

The next morning at 8:00 A.M., a small group of 15 Marines met at the Vietnam Memorial. The general did not attend. "He was too sick," his wife said. They would try and catch an earlier flight back home.

A former corporal by the name of Tim Hardwick had organized the ceremony and arranged for the wreath. Colonel Davis insisted that Hardwick and former Lance Corporal Jim Miller place the wreath at the memorial. They did so with pride as the others stood in silent homage to their fallen comrades.

It was Veterans Day, but a large crowd had not yet appeared at the memorial.

A gray, damp fog hung over the polished black granite, cloaking it in such a way that one couldn't tell where it started or ended. In this familiar setting so true to their Vietnam experiences, the men sensed the presence of those whose names silently appealed to them from the wall...invoking memories all too real.

Each Marine, in his own way, took in the magnitude of the happening. They had thoughts, many thoughts. Few were happy ones. They were the *what types*. What if their buddies had lived? What would they be doing now? What if the nation had seen the war through?

Many questions plagued them. None had answers. After several minutes, the gathering began to drift away like the encircling fog.

Two Marines remained, Jason Davis and Jim Flaherty. Jason sat on a bench facing the memorial. Jim slowly walked the wall, searching for a name. Finally he questioned a National Park Service Ranger. The ranger looked at a dog-eared list and shook his head. Perplexed, Jim started to walk away from the wall when Jason Davis called to him.

"You won't find his name up there, Jim."

Startled, he turned to Jason and sheepishly asked, "Whose name?"

"Lieutenant Kagan's," came Jason's mellow response.

"How did you know I was looking for his name?"

"Because you knew him better than I did, and he died on your watch. My barracks handled the casualty call. I knew him from my Vietnam tour right before I went to Boston.

"His name wasn't Kagan. He assumed it; took it from a draft-dodger. The real Kagan dodged the draft. The Kagan we knew was an Irish National by the name of Ned O'Shea."

Jim Flaherty, his mouth transfixed, slowly sat on the bench next to Jason Davis and stared at him.

"You won't find Ned O'Shea's name up there either," Davis continued. I did a lot of research on Ned after it came to light that he had assumed the identity of the coward from Boston.

"Among his personal effects, we found a diary Ned kept, telling of his experiences…a sad piece of writing, penned by a complex fellow. He was in the Irish Republican Army and had fled Ireland.

"When it surfaced that he'd replaced Kagan, the Corps went through the State Department for details about him. Irish authorities notified us that Ned belonged to the IRA, their number one hit man, and was 'on the run.' Apparently the British had a price on his head because he'd taken out a number of their troops along the border. He'd been in on a plot to kill a member of the Royal Family, but an inform-er blew their cover and Ned had to escape the country. He ended up in Boston through the Irish underground and as-similated into our society by taking the draft dodger's place.

"The State Department opined that it would be politically incorrect to include him among the names on the wall, so it's not there.

"Ned was an orphan. The Irish said he had no relatives. To the best of my knowledge Jim, history will leave Ned buried unknown at the Punchbowl in Hawaii. He's a forgotten man, and that's too bad because he was quite a man.

"Ned mentioned a Captain Parker in his diary. What ever happened to Parker?"

Jim Flaherty, now staring straight ahead, simply said, "He shot himself."

The two sat in silence before the Wall, each awash in a kaleidoscope of memories like waves at the sea shore, one after the other.

Jason Davis broke the silence. "Jim, some years ago I worked at the Pentagon. We lived in Old Town Alexandria. Everyday on my way to and from work, I drove by a Confederate memorial in the middle of town. It consisted of a Confederate soldier facing south from atop a granite base.

"Whoever sculpted it did a superb job because the figure casts a melancholy presence.

"One day I parked and went over and looked at the inscription on the base. It read 'They served in the consciousness of duty faithfully performed.'

"Somehow, Jim, that epitaph sounds appropriate for this memorial too."

Flaherty said nothing. He continued looking straight ahead, trying to reconcile in his mind what had happened to Ned O'Shea.

In their silence, a middle-aged couple and an older gentleman approached the monument cautiously and reverently. The younger man wore black shoes with rounded toes, dark trousers, a blue striped shirt open at the neck, a brown suit coat with wide lapels, and a maroon cap bearing the logo of a farm implement dealer.

The woman held the front collar of her faded blue coat up under her chin to ward off the dampness from the chilly fog. Springs of premature gray hair peeked out from beneath her head scarf. A well-worn black handbag hung from her left shoulder. She glanced back repeatedly, seeming to encourage the elder man a half-dozen paces behind them.

His steps were labored. He had on a frayed brown suit, and a dark felt hat covered his head. A skinny necktie, typical of the fifties, was askew at his throat. He carried something wrapped in green tissue paper in his right hand.

A park ranger approached and touched the brim of his hat as he greeted them.

They waited patiently as the ranger turned the pages on his clipboard.

He smiled, pointed to the trio's right, and continued down the memorial's pathway.

The man took the woman's arm and guided her in the direction of the ranger's gesture. The elderly man followed in measured steps, his eyes scanning the neatly-chiseled names.

Davis and Flaherty watched, and then heard the older man say, "Here it is."

The man and his wife moved quickly back to the spot where the old man pointed.

At that moment, the husband and wife surrendered their composure.

She fell sobbing against the black granite, her hand clutching, patting the name they sought.

The older man dabbed his eyes with a handkerchief as he tried to console them.

"They found their boy," Davis said, softly, almost rhetorically.

Flaherty nodded.

After several minutes, the couple unfolded some rubbing paper and traced their son's name onto it.

The mother folded the paper, as though she had just been given an altar cloth, and carefully placed it inside her hand bag.

She took the green tissue wrapped cone from her father, the man in the brown suit, and unwrapped a single rose.

Her husband removed a small roll of masking tape from his trouser pocket and taped the rose to their son's name.

The three locked arms as they stood there.

Silently, they walked away, arm in arm, disappearing into the fading fog.

Without a word, Davis and Flaherty got up and followed them.

-End-

GLOSSARY

adrift—Item not in its proper place.

all hands—Everyone in the organization.

ammo—Short for ammunition/ordnance.

Article 31—That article of the Uniform Code of Military Justice which prohibits self-incrimination

assembly area—Safe area where infantrymen make preparations to attack.

attack position—Last area offering any cover and concealment before infantrymen cross the line of departure

ARVN—Army of the Republic of Vietnam (South Vietnamese Army).

azimuth-horizontal angle measured clockwise from north.

bagged—Slept.

bangalore torpedo—Long cylindrical explosive device designed to blow an opening in protective barbed wire.

Bates Motel—Mythical setting for the terror movie, "Psycho."

bird—aircraft.

boat school—U.S. Naval Academy.

boot—New, unseasoned Marine.

bought the farm—Died in an aircraft accident.

bulkhead—Naval lexicon for wall.

bush—Tactical operations in rugged terrain away from a support base.

C rations---Combat food packaged in cans and plastic.

Canoe U—U.S. Naval Academy.

Charlie—Vietnamese enemy.

chopper—Helicopter.

claymore—Anti-personal mine.

company grade officers—2nd lieutenant, 1st lieutenant and captain.

Corps—Short for Marine Corps.

CO—Commanding Officer.

CP—Command post.

crapped out—Sleeping.

crew-served weapons—Ordnance requiring more than one person to properly operate it.

deck-Naval lexicon for floor. Marine vernacular for knocking someone down.

DMZ—Demilitarized Zone.

dope—Correct elevation and windage placed on rifle sights.

double time—Run.

Double unit of ammo—Twice the normal compliment of ammunition.

flick—Movie.

flipped him the bird—Make obscene gesture.

gooks—Pejorative term for Asians.

green—New, untried.

grunts—Infantrymen.

G-2—Division level intelligence officer.

hatch—Naval lexicon for door.

head—Naval lexicon for toilet.

heavies—Marine vernacular for higher ranking officers.

helm—Person responsible for leading an organization.

high port—Rifle held diagonally across the body.

HMM—Marine medium helicopter squadron.

hop—Ride in an aircraft.

hooches—Vietnamese grass houses.

Huey—Utility helicopter.

in country—Serving in Vietnam.

KIA—Killed in action.

ladder—Naval lexicon for stairs

line of departure—Point where attacking infantry come into view of the enemy

long sleeve sport coat—Marine vernacular for a straitjacket.

LST—Navy amphibious ship designated as a Landing Ship Tank.

medevaced—Means by which wounded personnel are removed from the battlefield.

military crest—Area forward and below the topographical crest of a hill.

mustang—Commissioned from the enlisted ranks.

Navy Cross—Medal for valor, second to the Medal of Honor

NCO—Marine Noncommissioned officer in the rank of corporal or sergeant.

net—Combat units using the same radio frequency.

non-judicial punishment—Offense not warranting a court-martial.

NVA—North Vietnamese Army.

office hours—Setting in which non-judicial punishment is administered.

old man—Vernacular for commanding officer.

1000 meter stare—The look on a spent Marine.

OV-10—Two engine Marine observation aircraft.

pad—Helicopter landing site.

passageway—Naval lexicon for hallway.

Pickled—Ordnance dropped from an aircraft.

Popular Force—Local South Vietnamese militia.

Project 100,00—Induction of Category IV B mental groups considered too slow for military service.

pukes—Rear echelon personnel in cushy jobs.

R&R—Rest and recuperation.

Richard Cranium—Pejorative term for the male member.

salty—Sailor or Marine who has faded clothing resulting from salt water spray—a veteran.

ship—Naval vessel or an aircraft.

S-1—Regimental or battalion level personnel officer.

S-3—Regimental or battalion level operations officer.

S-4—Regimental or battalion level logistics officer.

starboard—Naval lexicon for "right side."

rotated—Returned to the States.

rubber room—Marine vernacular for a padded cell.

saddle up—Strap on combat gear for immediate departure.

sapper—Soldier employing mines/explosives.

scuttlebutt—Naval lexicon for rumors originating around a drinking fountain.

Semper Fi—Short for Semper Fidelis (Always Faithful) the Marine motto.

skipper—The captain.

skivvies—Shorts.

spooked—Afraid.

stand down—Come off the line and relax in a rear area.

terminal grade—Last rank an individual will have in the military.

Tet Offensive—1968 general offensive launched by enemy forces against the U.S. and South Vietnamese troops.

tour of duty—Serving twelve months in Vietnam.

two-eight-zero-zero—Aviation term for 28,000 feet.

VC—Viet Cong. Enemy guerilla forces operating in South Vietnam.

VFR—Visual Flight Rules.

The Wall-Vietnam Memorial in Washington, D.C.

warning order—Alert for a pending military operation.

WESTPAC—Major command for U.S. forces in the western Pacfic.

WIA—Wounded in action.

wilco-Will comply.

willie peter—White phosphorous munitions.

wire—Protective barbed wire in front of dug combat positions.

zapped—Shot with small arms fire.

zeroing—Ensuring a rifle is correctly sighted.

0200—Military time indication 2:00 A.M. Based on a 24-hour clock, 1300 would be 1:00 P.M., etc.

Made in the USA
Middletown, DE
26 December 2019